Teaching Arabic as a Foreign Language

Teaching Arabic as a Foreign Language: Techniques for Developing Language Skills and Grammar is an indispensable guide for in-training and novice teachers of Arabic as a foreign language and a source of fresh and effective ideas for experienced teachers.

This highly practical guide outlines how Arabic second-language skills (listening, speaking, reading, and writing) and grammar are targeted in isolation from one another and how they are integrated to reinforce each other through the use of specific tried-and-tested techniques and activities.

Teaching Arabic as a Foreign Language provides instantly accessible, practical teaching techniques to target and develop specific language skills and grammar at novice, intermediate, and advanced levels.

Mohammad T. Alhawary is Professor of Arabic Linguistics and Second Language Acquisition and Director of MA in Arabic for Professional Purposes and the Teaching of Arabic as a Foreign Language Programs at the University of Michigan, USA. He teaches graduate and undergraduate courses on Arabic language and Arabic theoretical and applied linguistics.

Teaching Arabic as a Foreign Language

Techniques for Developing Language Skills and Grammar

Mohammad T. Alhawary

LONDON AND NEW YORK

First published 2024
by Routledge
4 Park Square, Milton Park, Abingdon, Oxon OX14 4RN

and by Routledge
605 Third Avenue, New York, NY 10158

Routledge is an imprint of the Taylor & Francis Group, an informa business

© 2024 Mohammad T. Alhawary

The right of Mohammad T. Alhawary to be identified as author of this work has been asserted in accordance with sections 77 and 78 of the Copyright, Designs and Patents Act 1988.

All rights reserved. No part of this book may be reprinted or reproduced or utilised in any form or by any electronic, mechanical, or other means, now known or hereafter invented, including photocopying and recording, or in any information storage or retrieval system, without permission in writing from the publishers.

Trademark notice: Product or corporate names may be trademarks or registered trademarks, and are used only for identification and explanation without intent to infringe.

British Library Cataloguing-in-Publication Data
A catalogue record for this book is available from the British Library

ISBN: 978-1-138-92099-6 (hbk)
ISBN: 978-1-138-92100-9 (pbk)
ISBN: 978-1-315-68667-7 (ebk)

DOI: 10.4324/9781315686677

Typeset in Times New Roman
by Apex CoVantage, LLC

To the dedicated teachers of Arabic to whom teaching Arabic is not a mere source of earning a living

To the persevering students of Arabic to whom all they have heard about Arabic being a difficult language means little or nothing despite often being made to learn too much in too little time

Contents

Introduction	1
1 Listening techniques	4

1 Developing listening at the novice level 4

   1 Repetition of sounds in single syllables
   تكرار الأصوات التي تقع في مقطع واحد *4*

   2 Repetition of sounds in context
   تكرار الأصوات في سياق *6*

   3 Listening to and identifying which sound is which
   الاستماع إلى الأصوات وتحديدها *6*

   4 Listening to and repetition of minimal pairs
   الاستماع إلى الثُّنائيات الصُّغرى وتكرارها *9*

   5 Listening to and repetition of minimal pairs and raising hand
   الاستماع إلى الثُّنائيات الصُّغرى وتكرارها مع رفع اليد *10*

   6 Listening to and repeating lexical stress on syllables with
   long vowels الاستماع إلى النَّبْر في المقاطع التي تحتوي على
   أحرف مدّ *10*

   7 How many words in an utterance? كم كلمة في اللفظ؟ *12*

   8 Listen and identify the letters of each word استمعوا وحدّدوا
   أحرف كلّ كلمة *12*

   9 Brief dictation إملاء قصير *13*

   10 True/false comprehension questions صواب أم خطأ *14*

2 Developing listening at the intermediate level 17

   11 Taking messages over the phone
   تلقّي الرسائل بالهاتف *17*

   12 Total physical response and carrying out commands
   الاستجابة الجسدية الكاملة وتنفيذ الأوامر *18*

viii   Contents

13 *Guessing game: what is it?* ما الشيء: لعبة التخمين 19

14 *Aural dictation cloze* ملء فراغات نصّ الاستماع 20

15 *Detecting errors: what are they?* ما هي: تمييز الأخطاء 21

16 *Filling turns in a dialogue* ملء أدوار حوار 22

17 *Dictation of a text* إملاء نصّ 23

18 *Picture ordering* إعادة ترتيب الصور 24

19 *Get the gist of the text* استخرجوا أفكار النصّ الرئيسة 25

20 *Complete the story: what will happen next?*
    أكملوا القصة: ما الذي سيحدث فيما بعد؟ 26

3 *Developing listening at the advanced level 27*

21 *Dictogloss* إملاء "الديكتوغلوس" 27

22 *Summarize in your own words* لخّصوا بكلمات من عندكم 28

23 *Jigsaw listening: listen and collaborate*
    الاستماع المُجتزأ: استمعوا وتعاونوا 29

24 *Comprehending the listening text in stages* فهم النصّ
    المسموع على مراحل 30

25 *Make up your own questions* ضعوا أسئلة عن النصّ
    بأنفسكم 31

2   Speaking techniques   33

1 *Developing speaking at the novice level 33*

    1   *Chain introductions and greetings* التعارف التسلسلي وتبادل
        التحايا 33

    2   *Name tags* شارات الأسماء 35

    3   *Match up* ابحثوا عن قرنائكم 35

    4   *Identity cards* البطاقات الشخصية 36

    5   *Describe the picture* صِفوا الصورة 37

    6   *My favorite day of the week*
        يومي المفضّل في الأسبوع 38

    7   *Group interviews* مقابلات جماعية 39

    8   *Who am I?* من أنا؟ 40

    9   *Describing family members* وصف أفراد العائلة 41

    10 *Fill in the blanks to personalize students in class*
        ملء الفراغات لشخصنة طلاب الصف 41

2 *Developing speaking at the intermediate level 44*

    11 *Memory chain* الذاكرة التسلسلية 44

    12 *Role-play* تمثيل أدوار 46

Contents ix

13 Guess what the teacher wrote خمّنوا ماذا كتب الأستاذ 47
14 What will you bring? ماذا ستحضِرون؟ 48
15 Marooned مُنقطِع السُّبُل 49
16 Interviews مقابلات 49
17 My ideal day يومي المثالي 51
18 Discuss and share تناقشوا وتشاركوا 52
19 What is the truth? ما الحقيقة؟ 52
20 120/90/60 or 4/3/2 تكلّموا أسرَع فأسرَع 53
3 Developing speaking at the advanced level 54
21 Picture-based story قصص مصوّرة 55
22 News reports تقديمات عن مقتطفات إخبارية 55
23 Group trip رحلة جماعية 56
24 Optimists and pessimists متشائمون ومتفائلون 57
25 Debating إجراء مناظرة 58

3   Reading techniques 60

1 Developing reading at the novice level 60
1 Spot the words البحث عن الكلمات 60
2 Sorting out words into lists تصنيف الكلمات في قوائم 61
3 "Bingo" سباق "البنغو" 61
4 Role-play تمثيل أدوار 62
5 Repeated reading aloud القراءة الجهرية مع التَّكرار 63
6 Fast reading القراءة السريعة 64
7 Sentence simplification تسهيل الجمل 65
8 Guessing then confirming التخمين ثم التأكّد 66
9 True/false comprehension questions صواب أم خطأ 67
10 Rearranging scrambled sentences إعادة ترتيب الجمل المبعثرة 68
2 Developing reading at the intermediate level 69
11 Getting the gist of the text استخراج المعلومات الرئيسة من النصّ 69
12 The comprehension race سباق الفهم 70
13 Guess the comprehension questions خمّنوا أسئلة الفهم 71
14 Guess the text خمّنوا النصّ 72
15 Recap and discuss more لخّصوا وتناقشوا أكثر 73
16 Reading fast القراءة السريعة 73
17 What is the advertisement for? عَمَّ الإعلان؟ 74
18 Information gap نقص في المعلومات 75

x Contents

19 3/2/1 لَخِّصوا وعبِّروا واسألوا 76

20 *Come up with the questions or summarize the text*
ضعوا أسئلة الفهم أو لخِّصوا النصّ 77

3 *Developing reading at the advanced level* 78

21 *Summarize in your own way* لَخِّصوا بأسلوبكم الخاصّ 78

22 *Retell a summary of the text* تبادلوا ملخصاتكم للنصّ 79

23 *Comparing texts* مقارنة بين النصوص 80

24 *Relating background knowledge and personal experiences*
الربط بالمعرفة السابقة والخبرات الشخصية 81

25 *I agree and do not agree* أتَّفق ولا أتَّفق 82

4 Writing techniques   84

1 *Developing writing at the novice level* 84

1 *Writing lists* كتابة قوائم 84

2 *Fast copying* النسخ السريع 85

3 *Planning an itinerary* التخطيط لرحلة 86

4 *Sentence modeling* النسج على منوال الجمل 86

5 *Writing a long sentence* إنشاء جملة طويلة 88

6 *Creative dictation* الإملاء الإبداعي 88

7 *Sentence completion* إكمال الجمل 89

8 *Rearranging scrambled words within sentences* إعادة
ترتيب الكلمات المبعثرة في جمل 90

9 *Similar and dissimilar* متشابهان ومختلفان 91

10 *Likes and dislikes* مرغوبات ومكروهات 94

2 *Developing writing at the intermediate level* 95

11 *Rearranging and modifying scrambled sentences*
إعادة ترتيب الجمل المبعثرة مع تغيير ما يلزم 95

12 *Brainstorming and fast drafting* استثارة الأفكار والإنشاء
السريع 97

13 *Transforming a dialogue into a narrative paragraph*
تحويل حوار إلى نصّ سرديّ 98

14 *My daily routine* نشاطاتي اليومية 99

15 *Personal letters, notes, and postcards* كتابة رسائل خاصة
وملحوظات وبطاقات بريدية 100

16 *Sum it up* اكتبوا الخلاصة 101

17 *Reconstructing a story* إعادة إنشاء قِصّة 101

18 *Completing a story* إكمال قِصّة 102

Contents xi

19 *Paraphrasing a text to simplify it* إعادة صَوغ نصّ
لتسهيله *103*

20 *Discussing job announcements/advertisements*
مناقشة إعلانات وظائف *104*

3 *Developing writing at the advanced level 105*

21 *Applying for a job in response to a job advertisement*
التقدّم إلى عمل بناءً على إعلان لوظيفة *105*

22 *Writing under time pressure* الكتابة تحت تأثير ضغط
الوقت *106*

23 *Differences and similarities* أوجه الشبه والاختلاف *107*

24 *Reconstructing the article from article outline* إعادة
صَوغ المقال من مخطط المقال *108*

25 *Whole class collaborative writing* الكتابة التعاونية على
مستوى الصفّ *109*

5 Grammar techniques 111

1 *Developing grammatical competence at the novice level 111*

1 *Chain question formation* صَوغ السؤال تسلسليًّا *111*

2 *Describing pictures using noun-adjective phrases* وصف
الصور باستخدام الصفة والموصوف *113*

3 *Find the relations between words* ابحثوا عن العلاقات بين
الكلمات *114*

4 *Chain question formation and the use of adverbials* صَوغ
السؤال تسلسليًّا واستخدام الظروف *115*

5 *Find related words by root and pattern* إبحثوا عن الكلمات
المشتقة من الجذر والوزن نفسيهما *116*

6 *Supply the definite article if necessary* أضيفوا الـ التعريف
في الفراغ وفق ما يلزم *118*

7 *Rearranging the scrambled words and making necessary
changes* إعادة ترتيب الكلمات المبعثرة مع تغيير ما يلزم *120*

8 *Translate the sentences into Arabic* ترجموا الجمل إلى
العربية *121*

9 *Sentence parsing* تحديد نوعَي الجمل وتحليلها *122*

10 *Identify the error, if any, and correct it* حدّدوا الخطأ إن وُجد
وصحّحوه *123*

2 *Developing grammatical competence at the intermediate
level 124*

xii Contents

11 Using the imperative and negative imperative استخدام
صيغتَي الأمر والنهي 125

12 Find your classmates according to their actions ابحثوا عن
زملائكم وفق أفعالهم 126

13 Compare yourselves قارنوا بين أنفسكم 127

14 Using the passive voice استخدام الفعل المبني للمجهول 129

15 Nominal sentence parsing تحديد الجمل الاسمية وتمييز
رُكنَيها مع الإعراب 130

16 Provide your reasons عَلِّلوا أسبابكم 131

17 Collapse into one sentence ادمجوا كل جملتين في جملة
واحدة 132

18 Name the structure in the text سمّوا التركيب في النصّ 133

19 Translate into Arabic ترجموا إلى العربية 135

20 Identify the errors, if any, and correct them حدّدوا الأخطاء
إن وُجدت وصحّحوها 136

3 Developing grammatical competence at the advanced
level 137

21 Dictogloss of a grammar point إملاء "الديكتوغلوس" لنصّ
يحتوي على تركيب معيّن 137

22 Complete the speculations أكملوا التكهّنات 138

23 Identify your errors and correct them حدّدوا أخطاءكم
وصحّحوها 140

24 Compare your attributes قارنوا بين خِصالكم 142

25 Identify the grammatical structures and vocalize them
حدّدوا التراكيب النَّحْويّة وأعربوها 143

Appendix A Correction symbols: intermediate level   146
Appendix B Correction symbols: advanced level   147
Bibliography and resources for further reading   148
Index   156

Introduction

This book contains five sets of 25 techniques, with a total of 125 techniques, aimed to develop the four language skills (listening, speaking, reading, and writing) and grammatical competence. Each set of techniques is loosely graded within each level (and numbered accordingly) and all fall along three proficiency levels based on the American Council on the Teaching of Foreign Languages (ACTFL) guidelines: the novice level (10 techniques), the intermediate level (10 techniques), and the advanced level (5 techniques). All the techniques are interactive and communicative in nature and are based on the communicative language teaching approach. Some are meant to target a particular skill in isolation, since it is extremely beneficial to do this at times, especially at the novice level. Others are designed to target a particular skill while integrating one or more skills so that class time can be optimally used and language skills developed in parallel. Ultimately, this integration is based on a well-known rationale of a sound integrated theory of language teaching, since skills are better developed when integrated, since they reinforce one another (e.g., Hammerly 1985; Alhawary 2013).

Each technique contains three sections: purpose, procedure, and variations. The "purpose" section explains the rationale for the technique, its learning or pedagogical objectives, its targeted skill, whether the technique is meant to be implemented to target a skill in isolation or being integrated to target more than one skill, and the approximate time it takes to execute the technique. The section on "procedure" offers a step-by-step explanation of how to implement a given technique. Many techniques whose application may not be self-evident, contain specific sample contents to illustrate how the technique is to be implemented. The section on "variations" offers additional suggestions of how the technique can be executed differently. Of course, there are many other possible variations with which any technique can be carried out, depending on the creativity of the teacher as well as their students' needs. In other words, it is up to the teacher to follow all the steps as suggested or to skip or replace a step with another one that they think will work better for their teaching style and/or their students' needs.

2 Introduction

A number of assumptions should be taken into account about the included techniques in general. These include the following:

- The overarching assumption of these techniques is to create classroom activities that are nonthreatening, fun, and engaging, including the grammar-based ones.
- Many of the techniques should be viewed as dynamic rather than static in that those designed for a certain skill can be used for developing another skill with modification if a proper focus is established on the targeted skill.
- Many techniques of a given skill can be reordered as long as the difficulty level of the targeted form and function are taken into account.
- The number of students suggested for each group work is not random but is always specified for any given technique so that all students in all groups can participate equally actively, all kept on task, and group-member dominance minimized.
- The approximate time suggested for a given technique to be executed is given so that the teacher can prepare accordingly and/or subsequent modifications of the technique are made with an eye on the time required to execute the technique efficiently. Some of the important dynamic factors here include the number of students in a particular class, the degree of homogeneity of their language background and proficiency level, the teacher's classroom management skills, and the teacher's ability to improvise and keep the pace of the technique going.
- The sample contents provided for some of the techniques are examples of how the techniques can be implemented and the teachers can use or develop different content to implement a given technique so long as the targeted language form and function are appropriate to the level.
- The Arabic variety used to illustrate the techniques here is Modern Standard Arabic, which can be substituted with any dialectal variety when (a) the content and context are appropriate and (b) the same variety is kept constant while integrating the skills; that is, integration is recommended to take place across skills rather than across varieties (see Alhawary 2013).

With little creativity, the teacher can modify any technique as they feel necessary to meet their students' needs and match their personal teaching style, select from them, or add to them other techniques to compile their own repertoire of techniques. It is hoped that each teacher teaching the Arabic language is dedicated to their profession. One manifestation of such dedication is being willing to compile one's own repertoire of techniques that they find most effective and best meet their students' needs. In this regard, and in addition to the entries of cited works as well as relevant works, the bibliography offers many valuable sources for further reading on techniques and crucially related topics.

Doubtless, there is a countless number of techniques that have been invented and reinvented, used, and reused with different modifications and variations. The techniques contained in this book are among the most effective, practical, and tried in the classroom based on the author's teaching experience of more than 30 years at the three different proficiency levels. Moreover, they require little to no prior preparation and are written and explained in a very accessible, straightforward style so that they can be readily used by all teachers of Arabic, the novice or in-training teacher, and the experienced teacher. In addition to being an essential resource for teachers, the book can be useful to draw insights for instructional material development and for in-training teacher preparation programs.

I am forever indebted to countless individuals who have contributed to this work in one way or another, including former students, colleagues, and all authors cited in the bibliography. My utmost gratitude is owed to Samantha Vale Noya at Routledge for believing in this project and for being exceptionally patient with me and my repeated requests for extensions due to many tough, unforeseen, circumstances. This book is dedicated to students and teachers of Arabic.

Chapter 1

Listening techniques

1. Developing listening at the novice level

Listening is viewed here in terms of the ability to recognize Arabic at the sound, word, memorized chunk, phrase, sentence, and paragraph levels. At the novice level, the focus is mainly on the sound, word, memorized chunk, and phrase levels. Towards the novice high listening is also pitched (a little higher than the ACFL guidelines) at the sentence level. It is both meant for sound and speech recognition as well as listening comprehension. Listening at the word level is generally useful for focusing on the sound level, whereas listening at the phrase/sentence level is helpful for focusing on how words are merged and heard together. A listening technique is usually implemented as a pre-listening, during-listening, post-listening activity, or all of these combined. Activities used during the pre-listening activities are usually referred to as "advanced organizers."

1. Repetition of sounds in single syllables تَكرار الأصوات التي تقع في مقطع واحد

Purpose

To provide learners with practice to perceive and produce sounds accurately. Imitation by repeating after the teacher or the teacher's demonstration of sound production is an effective technique (with many variations) to train learners to perceive sounds accurately. Repetition in unison is generally preferred over individual repetition, since the former has the added advantage of sheltering timid learners and the ability to test how well learners are perceiving and pronouncing sounds and words. The number of times for each instance can vary (1–3 times), depending on needs and control against boredom. Three times is usually a good cutoff point. It requires little to no preparation and takes about 5–10 minutes to execute.

Procedure

1. Read and have your students imitate you by repeating after you (1–3 times) the target sound in combination with the three short vowels, each syllable

DOI: 10.4324/9781315686677-2

separately or all three syllables at once, and then with the three long vowels—while pointing to each syllable on the board or screen as in the following samples of syllables:

Sample 1: ← بَ بُ بِ   با بو بي

Sample 2: ← تَ ثُ تِ   تا تو تي

2. When an emphatic sound (to an already-covered nonemphatic counterpart) is the target, read both pairs of counterparts with the three short–long vowel combinations (by pointing to each syllable on the board or screen) and have your students repeat after you 1–3 times. As in Procedure 1, each syllable can be read and repeated separately or all three syllables can be read and repeated at once as in the following samples of syllables:

Sample 1: ← تَ ثُ تِ   تا تو تي
           ← طَ طُ طِ   طا طو طي

Sample 2: ← ذَ ذُ ذِ   ذا ذو ذي
           ← ظَ ظُ ظِ   ظا ظو ظي

Sample 3: ← سَ سُ سِ   سا سو سي
           ← صَ صُ صِ   صا صو صي

Variations

Instead of first reading and having your students repeat a nonemphatic sound with all three short and long vowels before moving to read and have your students repeat the emphatic counterpart with the short and long vowels, read and have students repeat the nonemphatic sound with a short/long vowel and then the emphatic sound with a short/long vowel. In addition, each syllable can be read and repeated separately, or all three syllables (with short/long vowels) can be read and repeated at once as in the following samples of syllables:

Sample 1: ↓ تي   ↓ تو   ↓ تا   ↓ تِ   ↓ ثُ   ↓ تَ   ←
             طي   طو   طا   طِ   طُ   طَ   ←

6 Listening techniques

Sample 2: ← ذَ ↓ ذُ ↓ ذِ ↓ اذا ↓ ذو ↓ ذي
ظَ ظُ ظِ ظا ظو ظي

2. Repetition of sounds in context تكرار الأصوات في سياق

Purpose

To provide learners with practice to perceive and produce sounds accurately in words in different contexts and in different positions (initial, media, final). It requires little to no preparation and takes about 5–10 minutes to execute.

Procedure

Read and have your students repeat after you each word containing the target sound separately (1–3 times) as in the following samples:

Sample 1: ← سين سَبْت تَسْديد يَسْبَح دَبّوس جَلَسَ

Sample 2: ← شين شِبْر باشا بَشير ريش حَشيش

Variation

You can integrate listening with the reading skill by having your students read the words after the repetition is completed, each student reading one word in a chain fashion so that all students get to read the words.

3. Listening to and identifying which sound is which الاستماع إلى الأصوات وتحديدها

Purpose

To provide learners with practice perceiving sounds accurately, especially those that may be similar to others and learners tend to confuse between them such as the emphatic versus nonemphatic (such as ت versus ط, ذ versus ظ, س versus ص, and ك versus ق) and voiceless versus voiced (such as ث versus ذ, س versus ز, and خ versus غ) consonants in words in different contexts. Learners need to be reminded here to pay attention to the vowel quality of vowels occurring with such consonants: the back/heavy vowel quality occurring with emphatic sounds versus the front/light vowel quality occurring with nonemphatic sounds. It requires little preparation and takes about 5–10 minutes to execute.

Listening techniques   7

Procedure

Read (or play a recording) to class and have your students check the correct choice of sound they heard within a word such as Samples 1 and 2 that follow. Words comprising this technique can be based on minimal pairs as in Sample 1 but not necessarily as in Sample 2. Read each word separately with a short pause to allow your students to check the correct choice of the sound heard. You can read each word once or twice. Students should not be able to read the words, only listen to them.

Sample 1:
Teacher's Version

Check whether the word you hear contains ت or ط.

1-	تاب	ت	☐	ط	☐
2-	طاب	ت	☐	ط	☐
3-	مَتبوع	ت	☐	ط	☐
4-	مَطبوع	ت	☐	ط	☐
5-	بَتَّ	ت	☐	ط	☐
6-	بَطّ	ت	☐	ط	☐

Sample 1:
Student's Version

Check the box whether the word you hear contains ت or ط.

1-	_____	ت	☐	ط	☐
2-	_____	ت	☐	ط	☐
3-	_____	ت	☐	ط	☐
4-	_____	ت	☐	ط	☐
5-	_____	ت	☐	ط	☐
6-	_____	ت	☐	ط	☐

Sample 2:
Teacher's Version

Check whether the word you hear contains س or ص.

1-	صَباح	س	☐	ص	☐
2-	سَلام	س	☐	ص	☐
3-	مِصْباح	س	☐	ص	☐
4-	مُسْلِم	س	☐	ص	☐

8 Listening techniques

5-	ناس	س ☐	ص ☐	
6-	مِقَصّ	س ☐	ص ☐	

Sample 2:
Student's Version

Check the box whether the word you hear contains س or ص.

1-	_____	س ☐	ص ☐
2-	_____	س ☐	ص ☐
3-	_____	س ☐	ص ☐
4-	_____	س ☐	ص ☐
5-	_____	س ☐	ص ☐
6-	_____	س ☐	ص ☐

Variation

More than two such sound choices can be included, but perhaps not more than 3–4 maximum so students won't be distracted by the presence of too many words and the task becomes too difficult such as in the following sample:

Sample:
Teacher's Version

Check whether the word you hear contains ث, ذ or ظ.

1- ثُبات	ث ☐	ذ ☐	ظ ☐
2- ذُباب	ث ☐	ذ ☐	ظ ☐
3- ظُروف	ث ☐	ذ ☐	ظ ☐
4- مُذاكَرة	ث ☐	ذ ☐	ظ ☐
5- مُثابَرة	ث ☐	ذ ☐	ظ ☐
6- مَظالِم	ث ☐	ذ ☐	ظ ☐

Sample:
Student's Version

Check whether the word you hear contains ث, ذ or ظ.

1- _____	ث ☐	ذ ☐	ظ ☐
2- _____	ث ☐	ذ ☐	ظ ☐
3- _____	ث ☐	ذ ☐	ظ ☐

Listening techniques 9

4- _____	ث ☐	ذ ☐	ظ ☐
5- _____	ث ☐	ذ ☐	ظ ☐
6- _____	ث ☐	ذ ☐	ظ ☐

4. *Listening to and repetition of minimal pairs* الاستماع إلى الثُنائيات الصُغرى وتَكرارها

Purpose

To provide learners with practice to recognize phonemic contrasts and variations in order to help them develop proper perception at the sound level as well as the proper perception of the nature of vowels occurring with consonants and vice versa. In particular, the proper attention to the nature of the vowel quality (front/light vs. back/heavy) will lead to proper perception of consonants (emphatic versus nonemphatic ones). It requires little preparation and takes about 5–10 minutes to execute.

Procedure

1. Read words in pairs to your students and have them repeat after you (1–3 times) and have them pay attention to the phonemic contrasts whether these are *consonant phonemes* (i.e., emphatic vs. nonemphatic) or *vowel phonemes* (i.e., long vs. short) as in the following samples. If a word involves an emphatic, have your students pay attention to the back/heavy vowel quality occurring with emphatic sounds versus the front/light vowel quality occurring with nonemphatic sounds. When reading each pair, do so with a short pause between the two words. Your students can look at you or read directly from the handout, book, or board.

Consonants Contrasts

Sample: ساح صاح   سال صال   سام صام ←

صار سار   صور سور   صين سين ←

Vowel Contrasts

Sample: شارب شَرب   عالِم عِلم   سامِع سَمِع ←

Vowel Variation (and consonant contrasts)

Sample: تِفْل طِفْل   تول طول   تَرَف طَرَف ←

10 Listening techniques

Variation

When repeating after you, your students can look at you, away, or read words from the drill in the handout or book or on the board or screen. To make the drill more challenging, have your students look away from you and conversely.

5. Listening to and repetition of minimal pairs and raising hand الاستماع إلى الثُّنائيات الصُّغرى وتَكرارها مع رفع اليد

Purpose

To provide learners with practice to recognize phonemic contrasts and variations in order to help them develop the proper perception of sounds and vowels while energizing them if they look bored or tired. It requires little preparation and takes about 5–10 minutes to execute.

Procedure

1. Read to your students minimal pairs such as those in the samples above.
2. Have your students look at you and have them raise their right hands if the word they hear contains an emphatic sound (or long vowel) or raise their left hands if the word they hear contains a nonemphatic sound.
3. Read each word separately and observe their responses and repeat as needed until they hear and respond correctly.

Variations

a. Your students can look away from you or you look away from them (in such a way so as not to see your mouth when you pronounce the words) and follow Procedure 3 above.
b. To add fun to the activity, you can speed up and slow down your reading of the words.
c. You can also change the order of the words in each pair so that you do not start each pair with an emphatic in the first word but can start a pair with a word containing a nonemphatic sound as well.

6. Listening to and repeating lexical stress on syllables with long vowels الاستماع إلى النَّبْر في المقاطع التي تحتوي على أحرف مدّ

Purpose

To provide learners with practice to associate lexical/word stress with vowel length. Learners of Arabic, especially English speakers, often mistake short vowels for

Listening techniques 11

long vowels and long vowels for short. However, training learners to pay attention to lexical/word stress can help learners distinguish between short and long vowels in multisyllabic words, since stress in Arabic is usually associated with long vowels. Arabic word stress has many rules, but this one rule is the most helpful to know at this basic level for the purpose stated above. It requires little preparation and takes about 5–10 minutes to execute.

Procedure

1. Read to your students bisyllabic and trisyllabic words containing one long syllable, with stress on the long syllable to demonstrate long vowels versus short vowels (i.e., syllables containing long vowels vs. syllables containing short vowels) such as the following samples:

Sample 1
Bisyllabic words:
→ طالِب عالَم غُلوم بُيوت قَريب عَطْشان

Sample 2
Trisyllabic words:
→ مَدارس نَوافِذ سَيّارة قِدّيسة يُشاهِد يُقابِل

2. Have your students repeat after you (they can look at you or at the words away from you).
3. After reading each word, ask your students how many syllables the word consists of.
4. Then, ask your students where the stress falls by underlining or highlighting the appropriate syllable (i.e., containing *'alif*, *waa*, or *yaa'*).

Variations

a. You can skip Stage 2 (i.e., not ask your students to repeat after you).
b. You can pair words, especially those derived from the same root, which will add to the complexity of the task a little as in the following sample words (these can be bisyllabic, trisyllabic, or mixed):

Sample 1:
→ عَليم عالِم قَديم قادِم ضاحِك ضَحوك

Sample 2:
→ طَويلة طاوِلة قَديمة قادِمة ضاحِكة ضَحوكة

Sample 3:
→ طَويل طاوِلة قَديم قادِمة ضاحِكة ضَحوك

c. Have your students raise their hands as they hear the syllable with the long vowel.

12 Listening techniques

d. You can raise your hand with them to show them or guide them in the first reading and later offer feedback/correction with your hand as well.
e. Alternatively, students can be asked to mark (in writing) where they heard stress within a word.

7. How many words in an utterance? كم كلمة في اللفظ؟

Purpose

To provide learners with practice to identify word boundaries and identify separate words within an utterance. In particular, the activity provides learners with practice to identify definite words versus indefinite words and where words involve the eliding of the light *hamza* when a definite word is preceded by a word that ends with a vowel, short or long. It requires little preparation and takes about 5–10 minutes to execute.

Procedure

1. Read to your students utterances containing two and three words or more definite phrases containing sun and moon letters such as the following sample:

Sample: بابُ الْبَيْت   السَّلامُ عَليكُم   في الصَّفَّ   في الْبَيْت   تَحْتَ الشَّمْس ←

2. Ask your students how many words are in each utterance.
3. Alert your students to the clue of the *shadda* in the middle of the utterance, signaling the presence of a sun letter, versus the absence of the *shadda* and the presence of the [l] sound to indicate the utterance is definite.

Variations

a. Start the drill by reading to your students indefinite phrases so they get to be prepared for the subsequent definite phrases.
b. Alternatively, the phrases you read can be a mix of definite and indefinite phrases.

8. Listen and identify the letters of each word استمعوا وحدّدوا أحرف كلّ كلمة

Purpose

To provide learners with practice to identify word boundaries and identify separate words within an utterance. In particular, the activity provides learners with additional exposure to what counts as separate words (including particles such as

Listening techniques 13

prepositions, conjunctions, pronouns, etc.). It requires little preparation and takes about 5–10 minutes to execute.

Procedure

1. Provide your students with a passage of nonconnected letters with equal letter spacing among letters and words (written in a handout, on the board, screen, or via a document projector) such as the following sample:

Sample: أ ن ا م ن م د ي ن ة و ا ش ن ط ن ف ي ا ل و ل ا ي ا ت ←
ا ل م ت ح د ة ف ي أ م ر ي ك ا أ ع م ل ف ي م ك ت ب
ة ا ل ج ا م ع ة ه ـ ذ ا ع م ل ي ا ل ج د ي د ل ك ن أ ح
ب ع م ل ي ا ل ق د ي م أ ك ث ر.

2. Read and have your students draw a vertical line after each word until you complete reading the entire passage.
3. Divide students into dyads and have them briefly discuss their responses.
4. Go over your students' responses as a whole class.

Variation

Integrate this activity with the reading skill by having your students read the connected words after the activity is completed, with each student reading one sentence in a chain fashion so that all students get to read the words.

9. *Brief dictation* إملاء قصير

Purpose

To provide learners with practice to perceive sounds and words accurately. At the novice level, to control for the level of difficulty (since learners at this level are still learning how to write), listening is limited to utterances containing one or two words and to reproducing them (in writing) accurately so that the emphasis is placed on the learner's perception of sounds and words. It is important to provide instant feedback on the dictated items, right after the teacher finishes the dictation. It requires little preparation and takes about 5–10 minutes to execute.

Procedure

1. Come up with a list of 6–8 words or phrases, containing sounds that students have learned recently and those that are similar or challenging to them (i.e.,

14 Listening techniques

emphatic vs. nonemphatic sounds and short vs. long vowels); such words may or may not be minimal pairs such as in the following sample:

Sample:

2. سَحاب	1. صَباح	←
4. أَبَد	3. عَبَد	
6. غَريب	5. خَريف	
8. صاروخ صَغير	7. سور قَصير	

2. Ask your students to number their responses in writing accordingly.
3. Tell your students that you will be reading each utterance three times and that you will be exaggerating the reading the first time, less so the second time, and naturally the third time.
4. Instruct your students to write down all that they hear, including short and long vowels.
5. Have your students write down what you dictate in pencil so that they can correct a given response as they listen to it the second and third times.
6. Go over your students' responses as a whole class, by eliciting one word at a time and writing it down on the board as you heard it from students and then elicit corrections from other students.

Variations

a. Dictated items can be phrases or short sentences, depending on the need and level of your students.
b. Instead of repeating each item three times, repetition can be limited 1–2 times.
c. A student can dictate the words; corrections can then be made according to how the student has just read the items to class.
d. Have your students copy their responses on the board (with each student writing one item) and then elicit corrections from the whole class.
e. Alternatively, display via a document projector the written responses of a student or one response from one student at a time and go over them as a whole class.

10. True/false comprehension questions صواب أم خطأ

Purpose

To provide learners with practice to listen for meaning and develop their listening comprehension ability. Learners respond briefly and minimally through yes/no answers to short statements (recorded or read) about a short text, famous people, word meanings, or a picture. It requires little preparation and takes about 5–10 minutes to execute.

Listening techniques **15**

Procedure

1. Prepare short statements (recorded or read) about a short text or content of a lesson your students have recently covered, general facts, word meanings (e.g., synonyms, antonyms, plural forms, etc.), or a picture (such as the one displayed as Figure 1).
2. Provide your students with a sheet of paper with a blank column numbered according to the statements to which they will listen, each row containing a box for the true response and another for the false response to be checked where appropriate as in the following samples:

Sample 1:	**Students' Responses**		**Statements on Text**	←

☑ خَطَأ	☐ صَواب	.1	مُنى فِلَسطينِيَّة.	.1
☐ خَطَأ	☑ صَواب	.2	مُنى تَدْرُس الأَدَب.	.2
☑ خَطَأ	☐ صَواب	.3	والِدَة مُنى مِصْرِيَّة.	.3
☑ خَطَأ	☐ صَواب	.4	والِد مُنى أُسْتاذ.	.4
☐ خَطَأ	☑ صَواب	.5	والِدَة مُنى تَعْمَل في جامِعة.	.5

Sample 2:	**Students' Responses**		**Statements on Facts and Word Meanings**	←

☑ خَطَأ	☐ صَواب	.1	الطَّقْسُ في الصَّيف بارِد.	.1
☑ خَطَأ	☐ صَواب	.2	شيكاغو مَدينةٌ صَغيرة.	.2
☑ خَطَأ	☐ صَواب	.3	جامِعةُ هارْفَرد في واشِنْطن.	.3
☐ خَطَأ	☑ صَواب	.4	غالٍ عَكْسُ رَخيص.	.4
☐ خَطَأ	☑ صَواب	.5	شُبّاك يَعني نافِذة.	.5
☑ خَطَأ	☐ صَواب	.6	مَدينة جَمْعُها مَدينات.	.6

Sample 3:	**Students' Responses**		**Statements Describing a Picture (Figure 1)**	←

☑ خَطَأ	☐ صَواب	.1	رَجُل واقِف	.1
☐ خَطَأ	☑ صَواب	.2	امرأة تَمشي	.2
☑ خَطَأ	☐ صَواب	.3	في اللَّيل	.3
☑ خَطَأ	☐ صَواب	.4	مدينة قَديمة	.4

16   Listening techniques

Figure 1 © Shutterstock

3. Ask your students to check the appropriate box upon hearing each statement.
4. Follow the preceding step until your students have listened and responded to all the statements.
5. Go over the responses as a whole class or later by providing written feedback.

Variations

a. The format of the questions can alternatively be given as yes/no comprehension questions as in the following sample:

Sample:	**Students' Responses**					**Statements on Text**	←
	☑	لا	☐	نَعَم	1.	هَلْ مُنى فِلَسطينِيَّة؟	1.
	☐	لا	☑	نَعَم	2.	هَلْ تَدْرُس مُنى الأدَب؟	2.
	☑	لا	☐	نَعَم	3.	هَلْ والِدَة مُنى مِصْرِيَّة؟	3.
	☑	لا	☐	نَعَم	4.	هَلْ والِد مُنى أُسْتاذ؟	4.
	☐	لا	☑	نَعَم	5.	هَلْ تَعْمَلُ والِدَة مُنى في جامِعة؟	5.

b. Responses can be given by students verbally.
c. Go over your students' responses as a whole class and elicit corrections from all students.

Listening techniques   17

2. Developing listening at the intermediate level

At the intermediate level, listening is pitched at the sentence and simple speech/ paragraph level. At this stage, learners of Arabic will benefit greatly from continued listening practice in isolation. However, it may also be useful to sometimes implement techniques that integrate listening with one or more skills such as speaking and writing as is suggested in some of the techniques here. A listening technique is usually implemented as a pre-listening, during-, post-listening activity, or all of these combined. Activities used during the pre-listening activities are usually referred to as "advanced organizers."

11. Taking messages over the phone تلقّي الرسائل بالهاتف

Purpose

To provide learners with practice to perceive words, phrases, and sentences accurately. This activity encourages learners to develop self-confidence, as it encourages them to use Arabic outside of the classroom and employ it meaningfully. It requires little preparation and takes about 5 minutes to execute.

Procedure

1. Prepare a sentence for each of your students in the class and have them call you within a time frame that suits you and your students.
2. The sentences can be about anything and unrelated, or they can be related to a short story such as in the following sample sentences:

Sample:

1.   مَساءَ الخَميس اتَّصَلَت بي صَديقتي سَلْمى.
2.   قالَت لي إنَّها انْتَهَتْ من مُحاضَراتها في الجامِعة في السّاعةِ الثّانية.
3.   أرادَتْ أن تَرْجِع إلى بَيْتِها بالسّيّارة.
4.   لكِنَّها ما استَطاعَتْ أنْ تَسوق سَيّارتَها بسببِ حادِثٍ كبيرٍ في الشّارِع.
5.   فَقَرَّرَتْ أنْ تَمْشي إلى البيت.
6.   كانَ هذا أسْوَأ قَرارٍ في حياتِها.

3. Instruct your students to exchange the greetings with you in Arabic and then memorize or write down the sentence you read to them.
4. For each student who calls, read a sentence to them only once unless the student asks you to repeat it or asks you for any clarification (in Arabic) about a word or phrase
5. Have your students bring the sentences to class for feedback and discussion.

18   Listening techniques

Variations

a. You can choose to read each sentence to two students, especially if the class has many students.
b. In class later, have each pair of students who listened to the same sentence find each other to discuss their sentence before you go over the sentences as a whole class.
c. If the sentences are related such as having been taken from a story, have your students arrange their scrambled sentences into a meaningful story.
d. This variation will allow you to integrate the development of more than one skill: listening with speaking.

(See also Ur 1984)

12.   *Total physical response and carrying out commands*
الاستجابة الجسدية الكاملة وتنفيذ الأوامر

Purpose

Total physical response is sometimes referred to as an approach in its own right, but it is used here as a technique. It allows learners to attend to meaning and to show comprehension through their physical (nonverbal) execution of the commands they are told to perform. The comprehension check in this case is the correct (physical) execution of a given command. This type of activity can range from very basic commands, suitable for the novice level, to more complex commands, appropriate for the intermediate level. The activity can bring a lot of energy and fun to the classroom. The only possible disadvantage of this technique is that it is more suitable for young learners. For older learners, more appropriate commands can be designed to fit certain needs such as learning the numbers, for example, "open the book on page 35," "open the book on page 68," "open the book on page 11," and so on. It requires little to no preparation and takes about 10 minutes to execute.

Procedure

1. Give 1–3 physical commands to a student and have the student execute the commands in front of the class such as in the following sample commands:

Sample:

تَعالَ/تَعالَي إلى هُنا.

إذهب/إذهبي إلى هناك.

أحضر/أحضري كتابك وضعه/ضعيه على الطاولة.

إفتح/إفتحي الكتاب على الصفحة 173. أغلق/أغلقي الكتاب.

إرفع/إرفعي يدك وضعها/ضعيها على رأسك.

إرفع/إرفعي يدك اليمنى ورجلك اليسرى.

إمش/إمشي إلى الشبّاك وقف/قفي هناك.

Listening techniques **19**

2. The commands should be based on verbs and vocabulary appropriate to the level of your students.
3. For feedback or correction of an execution of a command, have another student execute the same command.

Variations

a. Prepare written commands on index cards/sheets of paper and place the stash of commands in a basket or bag.
b. Give your students commands according to what you draw from the stash of commands.
c. Have a student draw 3–5 cards and give commands to another student as you did.
d. The student should give the correct command inflected for the proper gender to fit the student executing the command (second-person singular masculine vs. second-person singular feminine); this variation has the advantage of integrating listening comprehension with the reading and speaking skills.

(See also Krashen and Terrell 1983.)

13. *Guessing game: what is it?* ‏ما الشيء؟ :لعبة التخمين‏

Purpose

To provide learners with practice to attend to meaning. Additionally, it allows integrating listening with speaking and allows for interaction in a meaningful and fun way. In this activity, the teacher describes something, and the learners guess what is being described. The description begins with the teacher giving only a little bit of information and then gradually revealing more and more information. It requires little preparation and takes about 5–10 minutes to execute.

Procedure

1. Come up with 5–10 salient description traits or clues of an object for guessing; the object of guessing can be a character, historical figure, thing, action, and so on such as in the following sample:

Sample: ‏خَمِّنوا: ما هو؟ (كلب)‏

1. ‏يسكن في البيت وخارجه.‏
2. ‏يمشي على أربع.‏
3. ‏له ذيل طويل.‏
4. ‏يأكل اللحم وأشياء أخرى.‏
5. ‏له أذنان كبيرتان وفم كبير.‏

20   Listening techniques

2. Allow time after each trait for your students to write down the information if they choose to.
3. Your students can guess whenever they feel they have been given enough information.
4. Reward the student who guesses the most items correctly.

Variations

a. Have your students prepare the 5–10 traits (about a character, historical figure, thing, or action) in class or outside of the classroom; this has the added advantage of integrating writing in addition to listening and speaking.
b. Have each student read the traits one at a time and follow the preceding steps.
c. Read the traits all at once and ask your students to refrain from guessing until they have heard all the traits.

(See also Ur 1984)

14.   Aural dictation cloze   ملء فراغات نصَ الاستماع

Purpose

To provide learners with practice to perceive words, phrases, and sentences accurately as well as listen for meaning. This is in a form of a cloze test or a short text with blanks to be filled in. To avoid making this activity too demanding, there should not be too many blanks (no more than one blank in each sentence or every 5th–7th word) and blanks should be confined to key vocabulary or new vocabulary of a given lesson. One added advantage of this activity is that it integrates speaking with reading. It requires little preparation and takes about 10–15 minutes to execute.

Procedure

1. Provide your students with a short, written text, containing blanks to be filled out such as in the following sample (with the underlined words representing the blanks):

Sample: أَنا خَليل أحمد علي، طالِب في كُلِّيَّة العُلوم السِّياسِيَّة بِجامِعَة قَطَر. اِلْتَحَقْتُ بِها مُنْذُ ثَلاث سنوات. وأَدْرُس لِلْحُصول على شهادةِ البكالوريوس. عِنْدي ثَماني مُحاضَراتٍ في الأسبوع. ولا أَعْمَل الآنَ لأَنَّ الدراسة في كُلِّيَتِنا صَعْبة جِدّاً. عُطْلَتُنا الأسبوعية تَبْدأ يومَ الجُمعة وتَنْتَهي يومَ الاثنين.

2. Read the passage to your students and pause naturally at the end of each sentence.

Listening techniques 21

3. Read the text a second time to allow students to correct their responses and/or catch up on what they may have missed.
4. Go over your students' answers as a whole class.

(See also Ur and Wright 1992.)

Variations

a. A recording of the text can be played instead of the teacher reading the text.
b. The first reading can be slightly exaggerated, but the second reading should be natural both in terms of pronunciation and speed.
c. You can pause a little before each blank to allow your students to guess the missing word.
d. A recording of a song or music or people talking can be played during the teacher's reading to create the effect of background noise to train students to get used to listening with background noise.

(See also Ur 1984.)

15. Detecting errors: what are they? تمييز الأخطاء: ما هي؟

Purpose

To provide learners with practice to listen for meaning. This is similar to the previous activity, but, instead of blanks, wrong words are provided, and students are asked to detect such words, depending on their understanding of a story in a lesson or a text in a given lesson. One added advantage of this activity is that it integrates speaking with reading. It requires little preparation and takes about 10–15 minutes to execute.

Procedure

1. Provide your students with a short, written text of a (recent) lesson, containing wrong words which are not marked in any way such as in the following sample (with the underlined words representing the errors):

Sample:
أنا خَليل أحمد علي، طالِب في مَدْرسة العُلوم السِّياسيَّة بِجامِعة قَطَر. تَخَرَّجْتُ فيها مُنْذُ ثَلاث سنوات. وأَدْرُس للْحُصول على شهادةِ الماجِستير. عِنْدي ثَماني مُعامَلات في الأسبوع. ولا أَعْمَل الآنَ لأَنَّ الدراسة في كُلِّيَّتِنا سَهْلة جِدّاً. عُطْلَتُنا الأسبوعية تَبْدأ يومَ الجُمعة وتَسْتَمِرّ يومَ الاثنين.

2. Ask your students to cross out the wrong word and write the correct one above it.
3. Read the passage to your students and pause naturally at the end of each sentence.
4. Go over your students' answers as a whole class.

22 Listening techniques

Variations

a. A recording of the text can be played instead of the teacher reading the text.
b. A recording of a song or music or people talking can be played during the teacher's reading to create the effect of background noise to train students to get used to listening with background noise.
c. Feedback can be given at the end of the reading or upon hearing the wrong word and students' responding to it with the correct word.

(See also Ur 1984.)

16. *Filling turns in a dialogue* ملء أدوار حوار

Purpose

To provide learners with practice to perceive a complete stretch of a turn in a conversation. It also allows students to attend to meaning, since it orients them to missing turns in a dialogue and/or predicting the missing utterances. The activity allows the integration of listening with reading. It requires little preparation and takes about 15 minutes to execute.

Procedure

1. Prepare and type a level-appropriate dialogue for your students or adapt one from their textbooks, containing questions and answers, leaving the latter blank, such as in the following sample:

Sample:

نور : مَنْ صَديقُكَ المُفَضَّل؟

مايكل : _____.

نور : مَتى تَعَرَّفْتَ إِليه؟

مايكل : _____.

نور : كَيْفَ تَعَرَّفْتَ إِليه؟

مايكل : _____.

نور : كَمْ مَرَّةً في الأُسْبوع تَجْلِسانِ مَعًا؟

مايكل : _____.

نور : عَمَّ تَتَكَلَّمانِ؟

مايكل : _____.

2. Read the dialogue to your students or prerecord it (reflecting the different voices of characters in the dialogue) and play it to the class.

Listening techniques 23

3. Read or play the recording no more than twice and have your students write down the words of the missing turns.
4. Go over the dialogue as a whole class after the second listening (while preferably displaying it to the class via the document projector) by having one student at a time provide their response to a missing turn and eliciting corrections from other students in the class.

Variations

a. Instead of the answer turns in the dialogue being the target of the dictation activity, provide your students with the questions as the missing information to be filled in as in the following sample:

Sample:

نور: ؟_____

مايكل: روبِرْت صَديقي المُفَضَّل.

نور: ؟_____

مايكل: تَعَرَّفْتُ إليه في الجامِعة، عِنْدَما كُنْتُ في السَّنة الأولى.

نور: ؟_____

مايكل: تَعَرَّفْتُ إليه في حَفْلَة لِلطُّلّاب.

نور: ؟_____

مايكل: نَجْلِسُ مَعًا ثَلاثَ مَرَّات في الأُسْبوع.

نور: ؟_____

مايكل: نَتَكَلَّمُ على الدِّراسة والواجِبات والمُسْتَقْبَل وعَلاقاتِنا بالآخَرين.

b. Have your students work in groups of dyads to reconstruct the missing turns.
c. Provide the full dialogue to your students to have them check their responses outside of the classroom.

17. Dictation of a text إملاء نصّ

Purpose

To provide learners with practice to perceive a slightly long stretch of discourse such as a short paragraph. It is more effective if feedback on this dictation activity is given immediately after the teacher finishes the dictation. The activity allows for listening to be integrated the writing and reading skills. It requires little preparation and takes about 10–15 minutes to execute.

24   Listening techniques

Procedure

1. Prepare a short paragraph appropriate to your students' level.
2. Ask your students simply to listen during the first (naturally paced) reading of the text.
3. During a second reading, read at a slower speed and ask your students to write down exactly what they hear on a blank lined paper.
4. Read the text a third time at a slightly slower pace than the first reading but faster than the second one and have your students check what they wrote from the second reading.
5. Go over the dictation afterward as a whole class, checking what your students may have missed or misspelled and eliciting corrections from all the class.

Variations

a. The three readings can be prerecorded with a voice other than yours with a pause of 10 seconds after each reading.
b. Instead of going over the dictation as a whole class after the third reading, pair your students up (in dyads) to discuss their responses and make corrections in a different color pen; this has the added advantage of integrating the listening skill with that of speaking.
c. Alternatively, give your students the dictated text to compare their responses with the text outside of the classroom.

18.   *Picture ordering* إعادة ترتيب الصور

Purpose

To provide learners with practice to listen for meaning. The teacher reads a story and students are asked to arrange a set of individual pictures sequentially according to how the teacher narrated the events. It requires little preparation and takes about 10 minutes to execute.

Procedure

1. Find a story appropriate to your students' level, preferably a story with which they are familiar.
2. Provide your students with a set of discrete pictures related to the events of the story.
3. Ask your students to arrange the pictures according to the events of the story as they listen to you narrating the story.
4. Slow down as you read the story and/or allow your students to listen to a second reading.

Listening techniques 25

Variations

a. Students can listen to a recording of the story.
b. The same pictures can be used for a different story (i.e., if the story is narrated with a different sequence of events).
c. Students can listen to the story a third time, as needed, or depending on the degree of difficulty of vocabulary and events of the story.

(See also Flenley 1982.)

19. *Get the gist of the text* استخرِجوا أفكار النصّ الرئيسة

Purpose

To provide learners with practice to listen for meaning at the global level. Global comprehension questions usually relate to who, what, when, where, why, and how. A suitable text can be similar in size and content of news sub-headlines and similar clearly structured text (i.e., with no implied main idea of the text). It requires little preparation and takes about 10–15 minutes to execute.

Procedure

1. Find a short text appropriate to your students' level such as in the following text.
2. Provide your students with key questions relating to the who, what, when, where, why, and how of the text such as in the following questions.
3. Read or play a recording of the text (do not provide the written text).
4. Provide the written questions to your students and have them go over them before they listen to the text.
5. Have your students listen to the text again and allow them to correct or complete the answers they supplied upon the first listening.

Sample: → قال وزير التعليم كريم السعيد اليوم إن موعد إعلان نتائج امتحان الثانوية العامة لهذه السنة لن يكون قبل شهرين من الآن. وأضاف أن ذلك ضروري من أجل التنسيق مع وزارة التعليم العالي وتحديد علامات القبول في الجامعات. وستعلِن الوزارة عن النتائج عندئذ في المدارس الثانوية.

الأسئلة:

1. مـا موضوع النصّ؟

2. مَن المُتَكَلِّم في النصّ؟

26 Listening techniques

3. ‏مَتى‎ ‏سَتظهر نتائج الثانوية العامّة؟‎

4. ‏أين‎ ‏سَتظهر نتائج الثانوية العامّة؟‎

5. ‏لماذا‎ ‏لَنْ تظهر نتائج الثانوية العامّة اليوم؟‎

Variations

a. You can choose not to provide the questions to your students before the first listening; however, providing the comprehension questions has the added advantage of focusing students' attention on the specific targeted information.
b. To mirror the structure of the text and make the activity easier, order the questions according to their sequence in the text (i.e., Question 2 before Question 1 and Question 5 before Question 4); however, this may make the comprehension questions too predictable and too easy to figure out.
c. Provide the comprehension questions out of order, although this may make the activity more challenging.
d. If a third listening is necessary, allow it; this will allow students to build more self-confidence and lower their anxiety.

20. *Complete the story: what will happen next?* ‏أكملوا‎ ‏القصة: ما الذي سيحدث فيما بعد؟‎

Purpose

To provide learners with practice to attend to meaning and integrate listening with the writing skill. In this activity, students listen to an incomplete story and are asked to complete it. To ensure students attend to the meaning of the dictated text, they must show (in their completed written portion) enough details related to the dictated text. It requires little preparation and takes about 20–25 minutes to execute.

Procedure

1. Find a short story or come up with a beginning part of a story.
2. Read the text of an incomplete story or beginning part twice and then ask your students to complete the text in their own way, linking the completion portion to as many details of the story they heard as possible (in about 10–15 minutes), such as in the following sample:

Sample: ‏ماذا سيحدث للجَمَل؟‎

‏زعموا أنّ أسداً كان في غابة مجاورة لطريق من طرق الناس، وكان له‎
‏أصحاب ثلاثة: ذئب وغراب وابن آوى، وأنّ رعاة مرّوا بذلك الطريق.‎
‏فتخلَّف جمل فدخل الغابة وتجوّل فيها حتى رآه الأسد . . .‎

3. Do not provide the dictated part/beginning part of the story written.

Listening techniques 27

4. Ask your students to add a title to the text.
5. Go over your students' responses as a whole class and reward students with the completed story that exhibits as much logical sequence of the plot of events and shows a connection to the details with the dictated part.

Variations

a. Prerecord the text, preferably with a different voice than yours, and play it twice.
b. Before going over your students' responses as a whole class, have your students work in groups of dyads to discuss their responses to give the chance to each student to refine their response; this has the added advantage of integrating listening with speaking and writing.

3. Developing listening at the advanced level

At the advanced level and beyond, listening is pitched at the paragraph and extended discourse level, where listening is primarily focused on meaning and content. At this stage, the more advanced the level of the learner, the more effective and practical (given time constraints and proficiency development considerations) implementing techniques that integrate listening with one or more skills, rather than focus on listening comprehension as an isolated skill, is. While getting exposure to a form or function through a skill, learners can activate it through another and achieve control or automaticity through others. In addition to the techniques included here, some of the techniques in the intermediate section can be used for the advanced level when the texts and topics used are suitable for the advanced level. A listening technique is usually implemented as a pre-listening, during-listening, post-listening activity, or all of these combined. Activities used during the pre-listening activities are usually referred to as "advanced organizers."

21. *Dictogloss* "الديكتوغلوس" إملاء

Purpose

To provide learners with practice to perceive sounds, words, phrases, and sentences in real time. The activity does also allow one to attend to meaning, since the activity requires the learner to reproduce the exact text which requires a certain degree of attending to or knowledge of meaning. In addition, it allows the integration of listening with speaking and writing. It requires little preparation and takes about 10–15 minutes to execute.

Procedure

1. Prepare a long sentence or short text at the level of vocabulary and structure of your students about a topic related to what they have covered in their textbook.
2. Read the long sentence or short text one time.

28 Listening techniques

3. Divide your students into dyads and have them reconstruct what they exactly heard (in about 10 minutes).
4. Go over your students' responses as a whole class and have your students compare their answers with what you dictated by displaying it on a screen or via a document projector.

Variations

a. If a short text is the content of the activity, read the short text twice, allowing your students to take notes of key words during the second reading to help them reconstruct the text.
b. To allow your students to reconstruct the dictated text faster, divide them into groups of 4 or more.
c. Alternatively, have one student come to the board and write the dictated text with help from all students in the class.

(See also Davis and Rinvolucri 1988.)

22. *Summarize in your own words* لخَّصوا بكلمات من عندكم

Purpose

To provide learners with practice to primarily attend to meaning, as learners are required to provide a summary of their understanding of a text (as an audio or video recording). It allows the integration of listening with the writing skill so that learners can receive feedback on their comprehension as well as writing. The technique mimics real-life situations in which we often need to know the gist of what we hear or watch. It requires little preparation and takes about 20 minutes to execute.

Procedure

1. Prepare a level-appropriate text for your students or select one from their textbook and record it preferably using someone else's voice, or find a listening text or video clip appropriate to their level or from their textbook.
2. Ask your students to listen to the audio recording of the text or video clip 2–3 times.
3. Allow your students to take notes of the most important details.
4. At the end of the second or third listening, ask your students to transform their notes into a short paragraph summary of what they heard (in about 10 minutes).
5. Ask your students to also come up with a title of the text.
6. Go over a sample of your students' summaries (by displaying each via a document projector) as a whole class and offer feedback and corrections as a whole class.

Listening techniques 29

Variations

a. At the end of the listening part, have your students work on constructing the summary in groups of dyads.
b. Have groups exchange their final summaries so that each group will attempt to provide feedback and corrections to both factual as well as writing accuracy of the paragraph of at least another group.

(See also Ur 1984.)

23. *Jigsaw listening: listen and collaborate* الاستماع
المجتزأ: استمعوا وتعاونوا

Purpose

To provide learners with practice to primarily attend to meaning, as learners are required to listen in carefully (through an audio or video recording) and then identify the missing information or piece together the full story verbally or in writing. Accordingly, it allows the integration of listening with speaking and writing, as students are required to collaborate together to complete the task of piecing together a full summary of a story, a full general idea about a topic, or a reconstruction of a dialogue in the logical order. It requires little preparation and takes about 25 minutes to execute.

Procedure

1. Divide your students into dyads.
2. Provide each group with an audio recording that represents a part of a story or text about a topic; the sum of all the recordings tells a full story, full texts about a topic, or full dialogue.
3. Ask your students to take notes while they listen to their portion of the story.
4. Instruct your students to listen to their recording no more than 2–3 times.
5. At the end of the listening and notetaking stages, redivide the students into groups of four or more to piece together a summary of the full story, a full general idea about the topic, or the full dialogue in the logical order, much like a jigsaw puzzle.
6. Go over samples of your students' responses, inviting corrections from all students in the class.

Variations

a. If it is not possible for all groups to listen to their respective recordings (such as when not all of them have computers, smartphones, or headphones), assign some groups to listen to their recordings outside of the classroom or in different locations.

30   Listening techniques

b. Go over your students' responses as a whole class by delegating a student to come to the board and have all students from all groups help the student write a summary of the full story, text about the topic, or dialogue in the logical order.

(See also Ur 1984.)

24. Comprehending the listening text in stages فهم النصّ المسموع على مراحل

Purpose

To provide learners with practice to attend to meaning by attempting to understand an audio or video recording (which can be a self-contained video clip, such as a short documentary film about a certain topic or a historical event). Understanding can include key ideas about its content and context at a global/broad level or at a subtler level. The technique allows for the integration of listening with speaking, as students are required to work in groups and then report and discuss their specific responses. Additionally, the technique exposes students to some strategies of how to approach such a text and attempt to decode its main meanings. It requires little preparation and takes about 40 minutes to execute.

Procedure

1. Pre-listening/pre-viewing (advanced organizers):

   a. State the topic of the clip by means of one word (e.g., You are going to watch a video about التلوّث "pollution," if the video clips is a documentary film).
   b. Brainstorm with your students what they know about pollution and write their main ideas on the board (in 3–5 minutes).
   c. Brainstorm what words they expect to hear associated with "pollution" (in 3–5 minutes).
   d. Point out vocabulary (including new vocabulary) critical to the text that your students may have missed (in 3–5 minutes).

2. First listening/viewing:

   a. Play the video one time.
   b. Divide your students into groups of dyads and have them answer general questions (e.g., What is the purpose of the video? Where was the video produced? When was the video produced?; in about 3–5 minutes).
   c. Have your students refer to the board and whether their answers correspond to the ideas on the board.
   d. Have the groups report to the class and discuss their answers with the class.

3. Second listening/viewing:

   a. Provide a few specific questions that require subtler or more deductive answers (e.g., To whom is the video relevant? What are the most important messages of the video? Was the video successful in conveying its message? Why?/Why not?).

b. Play the video for a second time.
c. Divide your students in groups and have them answer the questions for the second listening (in about 5–7 minutes).
d. Have the groups report to the class and discuss their answers with the class.
e. Responses are acceptable so long as your students are able to substantiate them from the video.

4. Post-listening/post-viewing:

a. Focus on the form and function of new vocabulary and (cultural) expressions.
b. Go over the new words and expressions your students may have inferred from the text.
c. Elicit your students' responses at guessing the meaning of new words and expressions you have preselected by playing and pausing the video around their respective contexts.

Variations

a. You may choose not to point out vocabulary (including new vocabulary) critical to the text that students may have missed in the pre-listening activities (and rely alone on the words and expressions that your students will come up with) and allow your students to infer them from the first and second listening/viewing.
b. As part of the pre-listening activities/advanced organizers, your students can look at the general questions prior to the first listening/viewing.
c. Play the audio/video a third time, if time permits for a third listening/viewing, depending on your students' responses and needs.

(See also Field 2008.)

25. *Make up your own questions* ضعوا أسئلة عن النصّ بأنفسكم

Purpose

To provide learners with practice to attend to meaning by attempting to understand a short audio or video recording about any topic appropriate to the level, interests, relevance, and needs of the learners. It allows for the integration of listening with speaking, as students are asked to work in groups to make up their own questions and discuss answers to questions made by other groups. It requires little preparation and takes about 40 minutes to execute.

Procedure

1. First listening/viewing:

a. Play the short (2–3 minute) audio or video one time.

32 Listening techniques

    b. Discuss as a whole class the general topic of the audio/video; that is, what topic is it about? (in about 3–5 minutes).

    c. Divide your students into groups of dyads and have them come up with their own questions, 1–2 questions by each group; the questions can be general (such as those related to what, where, when, why, how, etc.) or more specific ones (in about 7–9 minutes).

2. Second listening/viewing:

    a. Play the video for a second time.

    b. Divide your students into the same groups and have them fine-tune their questions (in about 5–7 minutes).

    c. Have each group ask the next group a question in a chain fashion so that groups can rotate in asking and answering questions.

    d. Invite other students from other groups to help answer a question if a group cannot.

3. Third listening/viewing:

    a. Play the audio or video 30 seconds at a time.

    b. If none of the groups asked a relevant question on the segment, assign groups to make up one question each and call back the groups to ask each other as done before.

4. Post-listening/viewing:

    a. Focus on the form and function of new vocabulary and (cultural) expressions.

    b. Go over the new words and expressions your students may have inferred from the text.

    c. Elicit your students' responses at guessing the meaning of new words and expressions you have preselected by playing and pausing the video around their respective contexts.

Variations

a. Depending on how your students respond to the activity, you may need to guide your students initially suggesting questions (such as the general and specific questions suggested in the previous technique).

b. Alternatively, if there are speakers or characters and interactions among them in the audio/video clip, invite your students to make interpretations about the speakers' personalities and relationships where they can share their beliefs and opinions about various issues and debate with their classmates about new ideas or controversial social trends. This has the advantage to pitch the discussion at even a higher proficiency level.

(See also Field 2008.)

Chapter 2

Speaking techniques

1. Developing speaking at the novice level

Speaking is viewed here in terms of the ability to produce language to meet communicative functional needs (of interpersonal communication) at the word, phrase, and memorized chunk levels. At the novice high level, speaking is also pitched (a little higher than the ACTFL guidelines) at the sentence level. At higher subsequent levels, it involves communication at the sentence, paragraph, and then extended discourse levels and ranges from the use of high-frequency vocabulary and structures to the use of low-frequency (and specialized) vocabulary and (more complex) structures (along ACTFL's proficiency guidelines, 2012). With the implementation of the various techniques along the proficiency scale, the development of the speaking skill should take into account a gradual increase in fluency, complexity, and accuracy (of pronunciation and grammar) of the learner's production.

1. *Chain introductions and greetings* التعارف التسلسلي وتبادل التحايا

Purpose

To provide learners with practice speaking and developing fluency. It also helps them develop basic interaction and functional abilities, such as introducing oneself and exchanging greetings. It requires little to no preparation and takes about 5–10 minutes to execute, depending on the number of students in the class.

Procedure

1. Arrange the seats in class in a semicircle (or two semicircles one behind the other, depending on the number of students in the class).
2. Stand or sit where the right end of the semicircle is to your right and the left end to your left.

34 Speaking techniques

3. Turn to the student to your right or left; if turning to the student to your right, model the exchange of introductions or greetings; for example, turn to the student to your right and say اسمي محمد "My name is Mohammad" and elicit the response تشرّفنا "I am honored" or أهلًا وسهلًا "Welcome."
4. The student turns to the student to their right and follows the same modeling by saying: اسمي آدم "My name is Adam" and receives the response تشرّفنا "I am honored" or أهلًا وسهلًا "Welcome" from that student.
5. The chain of exchanges continues in the same fashion until each student in class has responded to the introduction with the previous student and introduced themselves to the next one to their right.
6. In addition to exchanging introductions, any form of greeting can be exchanged and practiced in the same way as in the following examples:

Sample introduction and greetings:	تَشَرَّفْنا/أَهْلًا وَسَهَّلًا	←	إِسْمي جون
	صَباحُ الخَيْر/النّور	←	صَباحُ الخَيْر
	مَساءُ الخَيْر/النّور	←	مَساءُ الخَيْر
	وعَلَيْكُمُ السَّلام	←	السَّلامُ عَلَيْكُم
	الحَمْدُ لله/بِخَيْر / بِخَيْرٍ، الحَمْدُ لله	←	كَيْفَ الحال؟
	مَعَ السَّلامة	←	مَعَ السَّلامة

Variations

a. This technique can be used when teaching a new greeting or reviewing all the greetings students have so far learned, one greeting at a time goes through the chain.
b. If using the activity to review all the greetings, when you initiate the second greeting, start with the second student (rather than the first student again) and the third greeting with the third student and so on so that you can avoid starting with the same student each time.
c. For young learners (to make the activity more fun), bring a ball with you and toss it to the student to your left or right (with whom you model your statement and response) as you say صباح الخير "Good morning" and elicit from them the response صباح الخير or صباح النور "Good morning" when they catch it.
d. The student who receives the ball turns to the next student and says صباح الخير "Good morning" as they toss the ball to them, and the latter should respond back صباح الخير or صباح النور "Good morning."
e. The chain of exchanges continues in the same fashion until each student in class has responded to the greeting with the previous student and initiated it with the next one.

Speaking techniques 35

2. *Name tags* شارات الأسماء

Purpose

To provide learners with practice speaking and developing fluency mimicking a real-life situation. It also helps them develop basic interaction and functional abilities such as, introducing oneself and exchanging greetings. It requires little preparation and takes about 15–20 minutes to execute, depending on the number of students in the class to prepare the name tags for all students.

Procedure

1. Prepare name tags in Arabic for all students in class and have your students attach tags to themselves.
2. Have all students get up from their seats and walk around to mingle and introduce themselves to others individually.
3. When two students meet, one introduces themselves by stating their name and states a couple of things about themselves, such as the following: اسمي . . . "My name is . . .," أنا من . . . "I am from . . .," and أدرس . . . "I study . . ."
4. Pre-teach your students the vocabulary they need to express themselves before they start this activity.
5. Each student should try to talk to at least five students.

Variations

a. Have your students make their own name tags (in Arabic) on sheets of paper but provide tapes to them.
b. Students can read each other's name tags and initiate the introductions by means of rising intonation and asking a couple of additional questions, such as the following: اسمك . . . ؟ "Your name is . . . ?" من أين أنت؟ "Where are you from?" and ماذا تدرس/تدرسين؟ "What do you study?"

(See also Klippel 1984.)

3. *Match up* ابحثوا عن قرنائكم

Purpose

To provide learners with practice to improve their fluency in speaking. It also helps them develop basic interaction and functional abilities, such as exchanging greetings. It requires little preparation and takes about 10 minutes to execute.

Procedure

1. Prepare cards (or sheets of paper) containing matching expressions.
2. Hand out the cards to all students in class, one each.

36   Speaking techniques

3. Students must keep their card hidden and find their other half (carrying their matching expression) by walking about in class asking for it (initiating short dialogues) or simply saying their expression to each one they meet and figuring out their matching expression in the process.
4. Once your students find their other half, each pair exchange the expressions in front of the class.

Sample:	صَباحُ النّور	← صَباحُ الخَير
	وعَلَيْكُمُ السَّلام	← السَّلامُ عَلَيْكُم
	مَساءُ النّور	← مَساءُ الخَير
	تَشَرَّفْنا	← إِسْمي جون
	الحَمْدُ لله	← كَيْفَ الحالْ؟
	مَعَ السَّلامة	← مَعَ السَّلامة

Variations

a. Instead of using matching expressions, the technique can be used as a vocabulary activity using words and phrases.
b. It can be used as a vocabulary activity on single words, with one set of cards containing the (single) words in Arabic and the other set containing matching pictures or meanings of words in English, just as in splitting flash cards.
c. It can be used as an activity on phrases, with one set of cards containing nouns and the other set containing matching nouns as second terms of 'idaafa or adjectives as in the following sample.

Sample:	الخَيْر	← صَباحُ
	الأُسْبوع	← عُطْلة
	تُرْكِيّة	← قَهْوة
	عَرَبي	← خُبْز
	واسِع	← بَيْت
	قَصير	← رَجُل

4. *Identity cards* البطاقات الشخصية

Purpose

To provide learners with practice speaking and developing fluency. It also helps them develop basic functional abilities of asking simple questions and getting to know others and interacting with them. It requires little preparation and takes about 10 minutes to execute.

Procedure

1. Prepare index cards for your students to fill out with basic personal information about their classmates (e.g., their name, where they come from, where they live, their hobby, etc.) such as the following:

	الإسْم:
	الوِلايَة:
	السَّكَن:
	الهِوايَة:

2. Divide your students into dyads and distribute a card to each student and ask each student to get to know at least one classmate by means of interviewing/ meeting them and filling out the card in 3–4 minutes.
3. If your students have not learned question words, pre-teach question words/ particles such as ما "what," من أين "where from," and أين "where" or instruct and demonstrate to them to simply use rising intonation.
4. Have each student introduce their classmate to the class from the information they gathered from the card.

Variations

a. Ask your students to get up from their seats and intermingle.
b. Distribute three cards to each student to fill them out from three different classmates.

(See also Klippel 1984.)

5. *Describe the picture* صِفوا الصورة

Purpose

To provide learners with practice speaking. It allows participation with the least anxiety and pressure on a particular student due to the collaborative nature of the activity. It requires little preparation and takes about 10 minutes to execute.

Procedure

1. Come up with a picture for your students to describe, requiring vocabulary they have recently covered and appropriate to their level.

38 Speaking techniques

2. Display the picture to the whole class on a screen or via a document projector.
3. Allow 1–2 minutes for your students to look at the picture and think of 2–3 things with which to describe it.
4. Ask your students what they simply see, allowing one student at a time to say one thing about it, in a chain fashion so that each student eventually participates.
5. Allow your students to respond with one word, if that is all they can do, but urge them to use at least two words.
6. Provide error corrections by means of recasting after each student describes the picture and produces an error in pronunciation or grammar.

Variations

a. To make the activity less threatening, have your students write 2–3 statements that they want to use to describe the picture.
b. Allow your students to consult their books or notes.
c. Collect what your students have written and provide feedback and corrections later.

6. *My favorite day of the week* يومي المفضَّل في الأسبوع

Purpose

To provide learners with practice speaking and developing fluency. It also helps them develop basic interaction and functional abilities of expressing likes and dislikes and providing simple reasons or explanations. The activity allows the integration of speaking with possibly the writing skill. It requires little to no preparation and takes about 15 minutes to execute.

Procedure

1. Model for your students your favorite day of the week and then list (on the board or screen or via a document projector) other days in order of your preference such as the following:

1. الجُمعة: يَوْمي المُفَضَّل
2. الأَحَد
3. السَّبْت
4. الخَميس
5. الأَرْبِعاء
6. الثُّلاثاء
7. الاثْنَيْن

Speaking techniques 39

2. Ask your students what their favorite days of the week and make a similar list in no more than 2 minutes.
3. Divide your students into dyads and ask them to discuss their rankings and provide reasons for their rankings or why they typically like or do not like certain days in no more than 4 minutes.
4. Ideally, implement the activity when your students have learned how to express providing explanations or reasons; if not, pre-teach them key expressions, such as لِأَنَّ "because" and بِسَبَب "because of" and how to use them.
5. Go over sample responses of your students by having groups delegate a group member to report to class their group's rankings and reasons.

Variations

a. If time permits, have all groups delegate a group member from each group to report to class their group's rankings and reasons.
b. Following the conclusion of the speaking activity, have each student write a statement or two about each day, stating why a certain day is their favorite day and why they typically like or do not like certain days.
c. Collect the statements for feedback and corrections later.

7. *Group interviews* مقابلات جماعية

Purpose

To provide learners with practice speaking and developing fluency. It also helps them develop basic interaction and functional abilities such as asking simple questions to elicit simple information. It requires little to no preparation and takes about 10–15 minutes to execute.

Procedure

1. Write on the board (or display on the screen or via a document projector) the question particles/words مَن "who," ما/ماذا "what," أين "where," متى "when," كم "how many," كيف "how," and لماذا "why."
2. Divide your students into groups of 4–6 students.
3. Have each group delegate the role of the interviewee to one of them, with the rest being interviewers.
4. Allow interviewers 2–3 minutes to write as many personal questions (at least 6) as they can (by using the words on the board fronting their questions) about the interviewee, such as place of origin, number of family members, place of residence, hobbies, interests, favorite foods, and so on.
5. Have your students within each group alternate in asking the interviewee their questions in 5–6 minutes.

40 Speaking techniques

6. Each group delegates a group member to report to the class the information gathered about the interviewee.
7. Offer feedback and corrections on any patterns of errors students have made forming questions and statements/responses, eliciting corrections from class first.

Variations

a. Instead of having all groups ask personal questions, have each group ask a different set of questions such as those pertaining to the interviewee's house/apartment, car, job, hobby, and so on.
b. Allow your students to also include yes/no questions.
c. Allow your students to write at least six questions and the interviewee's responses to them.
d. Go over sample written interviews (containing questions and responses) by displaying them via a document projector and work on the identification and correction of errors collectively from all students in class.

(See also Klippel 1984.)

8. Who am I? ‏من أنا؟‏

Purpose

To provide learners with practice speaking and improve their fluency. It also helps them develop their interaction and basic functional ability to ask yes/no questions. It requires little preparation and takes about 10–15 minutes to execute.

Procedure

1. Prepare some cards or sheets of paper, each containing the name of a famous person whom most students in the class can recognize (e.g., an actor, politician, student, etc.).
2. Give each card to a student who will assume the name of the person on the card and who will start the activity by asking: ‏من أنا؟‏.
3. All other students in class ask the student with the card yes/no questions to figure out the name of the person in the card
4. Students continue to ask questions until they are able to guess the name.

Variations

a. You can assume the name of the person on a given card.
b. A student gets a response only if he/she asked the question correctly.
c. Alternatively, you may ask your students to prepare cards (outside of the classroom) with names of famous persons for use in a subsequent class.

(See also Sepulveda 2012.)

Speaking techniques 41

9. *Describing family members* وصف أفراد العائلة

Purpose

To provide learners with practice speaking and develop basic functional abilities of asking simple questions and soliciting basic information. It also helps them improve their fluency, as it allows them to think of and rehearse what they want to talk about before the actual task. It requires little to no preparation and takes about 10–15 minutes to execute, depending on the number of students in the class.

Procedure

1. Have your students bring three pictures of their family members each.
2. In class, each student describes their family members (portrayed in the pictures) to the class.
3. The student describing the pictures is not allowed to read from notes.
4. After each student completes their description of their three family members, students in class ask the student questions (each student is required to ask at least one question) soliciting more information about their family members they have just described, such as the following:

- كم عمره/ها؟
- أين يسكن/تسكن؟
- ماذا يدرس/تدرس؟
- أين يدرس/تدرس؟
- ماذا يعمل/تعمل؟
- أين يعمل/تعمل؟
- ما هوايته/هوايتها؟
- ما أكلته/أكلتها المفضلة؟
- كم لغة يتكلم؟/تتكلم؟

Variations

a. Depending on the level of your students in class, prepare, if necessary, the questions for your students on cards to use in their questioning.
b. Students can also ask yes/no questions.

10. *Fill in the blanks to personalize students in class* ملء الفراغات لشخصنة طلاب الصفَ

Purpose

To provide learners with practice speaking as well as improve their fluency, as it allows them to translate what the teacher is prompting them by modifying each

42 Speaking techniques

fill-in-the-blank statement to personalize them in the drill while paying attention to both pronunciation and grammar. It requires little to no preparation and takes about 10–15 minutes to execute, depending on the number of questions in the fill-in-the-blank drill in the textbook. This also makes such a mechanical drill engaging and fun.

Procedure

1. Use any fill-in-the-blank drill in your students' textbook, preferably after having assigned it as a homework assignment, such as the following:

١. أسرتي صغيرة. لي أخ واحد ــــــــــــــــ . اسمه جون.

٢. لا أحب هذه المدينة ــــــــــــــــ الازدِحام.

٣. في فلوريدا الطقس ــــــــــــــــ في الشتاء و ــــــــــــــــ في الصيف.

٤. أحب السَّفَر إلى ميشيغان في الصيف بسبب الطقس الـ ــــــــــــــــ .

٥. سافر والدها إلى المغرب؛ فهي تشعر بـ ــــــــــــــــ .

2. Start by having a student read out the entire first statement with the missing word supplied.
3. If the supplied word is not the right one, elicit correction from other students in class.
4. Personalize the statement by making all possible (gradual) modifications to the original one and recycling recently learned words to be about some of the students or elsewhere as applicable by asking all class to translate aloud in unison, including you, the English version of how you are recasting it to be about specific students or other referents, as in the following examples of the first three statements of the drill (note: you can invent certain things, such as names of students' relatives):

Said by the Teacher		Said by all students and the teacher in unison
كيف نقول: Jessica's family is small. She has one brother only. His name is John.	→	١. أسرة جسيكا صغيرة. لها أخ واحد <u>فقط</u>. اسمه جون.
كيف نقول: David's family is small. He has one sister only. Her name is Sally.	→	أسرة داود صغيرة. له أخت واحدة فقط. اسمها سالي.

Speaking techniques 43

أسرتنا صغيرة. لنا عمة واحدة فقط. اسمها كيلي. → كيف نقول:
Our family is small. We have one paternal aunt only. Her name is Kelley.

أسرتهم صغيرة. لهم خال واحدة فقط. اسمه جو. → كيف نقول:
Their family is small. They have one maternal uncle only. His name is Joe.

أسرتي صغيرة. لي جد واحد فقط. اسمه سام. → كيف نقول:
My family is small. I have one grandfather only. His name is Sam.

2. لا يحب جاك هذه المدينة بسبب الازدِحام. → كيف نقول:
Jack doesn't like this city because of the crowded traffic.

لا تحب سالي هذه المدينة بسبب الازدِحام. → كيف نقول:
Sally doesn't like this city because of the crowded traffic.

لا نحب هذه المدينة بسبب الطقس. → كيف نقول:
We don't like this city because of the weather.

لا يحبون هذه المدينة بسبب الرطوبة. → كيف نقول:
They don't like this city because of the humidity.

لا تحبون هذه المدينة بسبب الطقس البارد. → كيف نقول:
You all don't like this city because of the cold weather.

3. في أريزونا الطقس دافئ في الشتاء وحار في الصيف. → كيف نقول:
In Arizona the weather is warm in Winter and hot in the Summer.

في تكساس الطقس بارد في الشتاء ورطب في الصيف. → كيف نقول:
In Texas the weather is cold in Winter and humid in the Summer.

44 Speaking techniques

في سورية الطقس بارد في الشتاء وحار → كيف نقول:
في الصيف.

In Syria the weather is cold
in Winter and hot in the
Summer.

في ميشيغان الطقس بـارد في الشتاء → كيف نقول:
ومعتدل في الصيف.

In Michigan the weather is
cold in Winter and moderate
in the Summer.

في الصحراء الطقس حار في النهار وبارد → كيف نقول:
في الليل.

In the desert the weather is hot
in the day and cold in the night.

Variations

a. Display the English statements (on slides or via a document projector) so your students can also see each statement written while they attempt at translating it into Arabic.
b. To make the class more energetic and to integrate writing into the activity, prior to the activity divide the board into columns according to the number of the questions of the fill-in-the-blanks drill.
c. Have a similar number of students go to the board so that each will write the missing word in the blank for a given question.
d. If there is any correction, write the correct word next to the wrong word in its proper column on the board, after eliciting the correction from other students in class.
e. Repeat this activity once every lesson or unit or when there is a fill-in-the-blank drill to activate the new vocabulary.

2. Developing speaking at the intermediate level

At the intermediate level, speaking involves communication at the sentence and paragraph levels. At the intermediate stage, learners of Arabic will benefit greatly from continued speaking practice in isolation. However, it may also be useful at times to implement techniques that integrate speaking with one or more skills as is done in some of the techniques here.

11. Memory chain الذاكرة التسلسلية

Purpose

To provide learners with practice speaking. It also allows learners to improve their fluency as well as accuracy by allowing them to repeat previously produced

Speaking techniques 45

sentences and focus on grammatical accuracy. Teachers (and other students in the class) are able to provide instant feedback and error correction through recasting (i.e., by reproducing the erroneous utterance without the errors). It requires little to no preparation and takes about 15 minutes to execute. The technique allows the integration of speaking with the listening (as well as possibly the writing) skills, as students are required to listen carefully to and repeat what their classmates have said.

Procedure

1. Prepare a list of vocabulary items selected from recent lessons or new vocabulary list from a recently completed lesson from your students' textbook so that your students can make up a story (based on the provided words) about anyone (i.e., anyone imagined or real, in class or outside of the class).
2. Display the list to the class on a screen or via a document projector and hide the list, showing one word at a time when each student attempts to use that word in a sentence to contribute to the collective story.
3. Start by asking a student to make up a sentence based on the first word on top of the list you show to start the first sentence of a story about anyone (i.e., the first student can determine whom the story will be about).
4. Ask a second student sitting next to the previous one (in a chain fashion) to repeat the sentence that the previous student produced, and then uncover the word down the list so the current student will make up a sentence based on the shown word to further contribute to making up the story.
5. Ask a third student next to the second student to repeat the sentences produced by the first student and that by the second student (in the same order), and then uncover the third word down the list so the third student can make up their own sentence to further contribute to the same story.
6. Follow the same previous steps until all words are covered and your students have made a sentence on each word on the list.
7. Help the student make up their sentence by completing part of the sentence or soliciting other students to help and using recasting to provide the student with corrections to their sentence.
8. To control the pace of the activity, for each subsequent student, start by covering the whole list and uncover one word at a time so that you can refocus on each word and your students can repeat the previous sentences made up by their classmates and then make up their own.
9. To further facilitate the pace of the activity and keep all students on task, have your students who constructed their own sentences be attentive and responsible for helping the student performing their turn to recall their sentences.
10. Students are not allowed to take notes or write anything; if they have not heard a student well, they need to relisten as each sentence will be repeated more than once later.

46 Speaking techniques

Sample:

← Student 1	سورئ →	
← Student 2	أسكنُ	
← Student 3	والدى	
← Student 4	يَعْمَل	
← Student 5	في	
← Student 6	والدَتي	
← Student 7	تَعْمَل	
← Student 8	أدْرُس	
← Student 9	نَفْس الـ	

Student 1 → ليلى **سوريَّة**.

Student 2 → ليلى سوريَّة. **تَسْكُنُ** في مدينة ديترويت في ولاية ميشيغان.

Student 3 → ليلى سوريَّة. تَسْكُن في مدينة ديترويت في ولاية ميشيغان. **والد** لينا أستاذ.

Student 4 → ليلى سوريَّة. تَسْكُن في مدينة ديترويت في ولاية ميشيغان. والد لينا أستاذ. **يَعْمَل** في جامعة ميشيغان.

Student 5 → . . .

Student 6 → . . .

Student 7 → . . .

Student 8 → . . .

Student 9 → . . .

Variations

a. If the list is too long, break it up into two lists so that students can make up two separate stories; this will also make the activity go faster.
b. After the activity is concluded, divide your students into groups and have them recall and write down their story in no more than 5–7 minutes.
c. Alternatively, have each student recall and write down the story to be collected for written feedback and corrections later.

12. *Role-play* تمثيل أدوار

Purpose

To provide learners with practice speaking and develop their speaking fluency as they are required to rehearse their acting roles for actual interaction later. It requires no preparation and takes about 20–25 minutes to execute. It allows for the integration of speaking with listening, since it requires an interlocutor with whom to speak.

Procedure

1. Assign a dialogue covered in class recently in the textbook.
2. Divide your students into groups according to the number of characters in the dialogue.

Speaking techniques   47

3. Ask your students to modify the dialogue as they wish and ask them to practice their dialogues within their groups (in 10 minutes).
4. Rotate among the groups and provide help as necessary and recast errors if heard.
5. Have the groups perform their dialogues in front of the class without reading from notes.
6. Reserve feedback and corrections of group performance until after the groups performed their dialogue skits and do so indirectly (going over errors you heard).

Variations

a. If there is no dialogue in a given lesson, choose a narrative text and ask your students to transform the text into a dialogue at home (i.e., as a homework assignment). In class, divide your students into groups and have them rehearse the dialogues they had worked on at home (in 5–7 minutes) before performing them in front of the class.
b. If there is a dialogue-related activity such as "Ask your classmates," have your students transform the activity into a meaningful, coherent dialogue, making changes where necessary, and follow the same procedure.

13.   Guess what the teacher wrote
خمّنوا ماذا كتب الأستاذ

Purpose

To provide learners with practice speaking. It requires no preparation and takes about 5–10 minutes to execute. It allows for the integration of speaking with listening, as it requires interaction between a student, on one hand, and all other students in class, on the other. It is a confidence builder as the focus is on communication to figure out the thing and not on the person speaking per se.

Procedure

1. Call on a student or for a volunteer to stand in front of the class with their back to the board.
2. Write something on the board, such as the name of a famous person (e.g., an actor or politician), an object (e.g., a car, a table, a building), or a vocabulary item (e.g., a verb or an adjective).
3. Students in the class help the student identify the object by giving the student clues.
4. The student can also ask the class yes/no questions to help them identify the object.
5. Reserve feedback and corrections until after the activity is completed.

48 Speaking techniques

Variations

a. Prepare clues on cards and hand them out to your students to help speed up the pace of the activity.
b. To ensure all students participate in the activity, have your students offer their clues in a chain one after the other.

(See also Ur and Wright 1992; Sepulveda 2012.)

14. *What will you bring?* ماذا ستحضِرون؟

Purpose

To provide learners with practice speaking. It also allows the improvement of fluency and lowers anxiety, as learners find themselves distracted by focusing on the task at hand and what they need to bring with them to a pleasurable trip. It requires little preparation and takes about 15 minutes to execute.

Procedure

1. Come up with a specific scenario for a trip to a specific location such as students are about to make a trip to the mountains, a trip to the beach, or a trip to the desert, among others.
2. Prepare a set of pictures of items that can be brought on such a trip.
3. Divide your students into groups.
4. Ask your students to select five pictures.
5. Have your students within each group describe the pictures of the items and their reasons for selecting them.
6. Have a student of each group report to the class the choice of their group's selection of the five items and the reasons for their selection.
7. Reserve feedback and corrections until after the activity is completed.

Variations

a. Include pictures of items that won't be helpful to bring to the trip.
b. Ask your students to select three pictures of items they will need to bring with them and three pictures of items they won't need on the trip.
c. Have your students within each group describe the pictures of the items and their reasons for selecting to bring the three items and reasons for not bringing the other three items.
d. Discuss and vote as a whole class for the group with the most successful choice for inclusion and exclusion of the items.
e. You can also ask your students to rank order the items in importance and provide reasons why.

Speaking techniques   49

15.   *Marooned* مُنْقَطِع السُّبُل

Purpose

To provide learners with practice speaking. It also allows the improvement of fluency and lowers anxiety, as learners find themselves distracted by focusing on the task at hand while they think of a solution to a situation and provide reasons why they have chosen a particular solution. It requires little to no preparation and takes about 15 minutes to execute.

Procedure

1. Come up with a task-based topic, such as asking your students:

   • If you were to be marooned on an island, what are five items you would bring with you, and why?
   • If you were to be lost in the desert, what are five items you would bring with you, and why?
   • If you were to leave for a trip to the mountains and camp there, what are five items you would bring with you, and why?
   • If you were to leave for a trip to the beach, what are five items you would bring with you, and why?
   • if you were to listen to three types of music, what would these be, and why?

2. Divide your students into groups of 3–5 and have them within each group discuss the items and come up with a consensus as a group.
3. Redivide your students into groups of 3–5 comprising one member of the previous groups and have them compare what their previous groups have chosen and why.
4. Reserve feedback and corrections until after the activity is completed.

Variations

a. Implement this technique after you have taught the conditional sentences.
b. Alternatively, pre-teach the conditional sentences before you implement this technique and have your students observe use of the proper conditional sentence structure.
c. Discus and vote as a whole class on the most important five items.
d. You can also ask your students to rank order the items in importance and provide reasons why.

(See also Klippel 1984; Vernon 2012.)

16.   *Interviews* مقابلات

Purpose

To provide learners with practice speaking and improving fluency, as they engage in rehearsal for interaction in real-life contexts. It allows for the integration of

50 Speaking techniques

speaking with listening and writing, as it requires learners to listen when being asked and write up the questions in preparation for conducting the interview. It requires little to no preparation. Each interview takes about 5 minutes to execute.

Procedure

1. Assign your students a topic for an interview as a homework assignment, such as interviewing a job candidate, interviewing a famous person, and getting to know their attitudes toward things (i.e., likes and dislikes), interviewing a student for admission, and so on.
2. Students should already be familiar with key vocabulary pertaining to the topic of the interview. If not, provide your students with a supplemental vocabulary of key words. For example, if the topic is to interview a job candidate, they should know words such as يتقدم بطلب للحصول "job," وظيفة "company," شركة "apply for a job," على وظيفة "qualifications," مؤهلات and خبرة "experience."
3. Ask each student to prepare a list of the questions to use (as the interviewer) with another student in class during the interview, which may include answers to what, who, when, where, how, and why.
4. Ask your students to rehearse possible answers for their questions so that they are ready to answer similar questions posed by their classmates when they are interviewees.
5. In class, divide your students into dyads and allow them to practice their interviews before conducting the interviews (within their own groups) in front of the class (in 5 minutes).
6. Collect the interview questions for correction and grading.

Sample:

1. أَهْلًا وَسَهْلًا. إِسْمي جون سميث.

2. (هل) أنتَ هُنا للمُقابَلة للحُصول على وَظيفة في هذِهِ الشَّرِكة؟

3. أين دَرَسْت ومتى تَخَرَّجْت؟

4. ما مُؤَهِّلاتُك الأُخْرى؟

5. ما خِبرَتُك؟

6. ماذا عَمِلْت في الماضي وماذا تَعْمَل الآن؟

7. لماذا تَرْغَب في الحُصول على وَظيفة في شَرِكَتِنا؟

8. كَيْفَ عَرَفْت عن الوَظيفة؟

9. شُكْرًا. (هل) عِنْدَك أَسْئِلة لنا؟

Speaking techniques 51

Variations

a. Have your students write up answers to their interview questions (based on the outcome of the interviews with their classmates) next to the questions and collect the interview questions and answers for correction and feedback.
b. Vote for the best interview.
c. Make this activity take place entirely in the classroom by having prepared a list of interview questions for students to choose from—with each group/dyad (consisting of an interviewer and interviewee) choosing 5–7 questions—and follow the same procedure.

17. *My ideal day* يومي المثالي

Purpose

To provide learners with practice speaking and allow them to improve their speaking fluency as they rehearse before they speak. It allows for speaking to be integrated with the writing skill. It requires no preparation and takes about 35 minutes to execute, depending on the number of students in the class.

Procedure

1. Ask each student to write down the daily routine of their ideal day from the morning when they wake up to the evening when they sleep (8–10 activities; in 8–10 minutes).
2. Divide your students into dyads to discuss the similarities and differences between their ideal days (in 10 minutes).
3. Have each group report their findings to the class: one student reports the similarities, and the other reports the differences.

Variations

a. Other topics include the ideal car, the ideal house, the ideal, university, the ideal friend, and so on.
b. Instead of having groups report their discussions to class, redivide your students into groups so that each student partners with a new student to discuss the similarities and differences of the daily ideal daily routine (in 5 minutes).
c. Repeat the process one more time so that each student has discussed their ideal daily routine with three students.
d. Have each student finalize a written narrative of their ideal daily routine in a paragraph (about 150 words), using different connectors, not just the conjunction و "and" (in 8–10 minutes).
e. Collect the written paragraphs for feedback and corrections later.

52 Speaking techniques

18. *Discuss and share* تناقشوا وتشاركوا

Purpose

To provide learners with practice speaking. It also allows learners to improve their speaking fluency and lower anxiety, as learners are able to rehearse what they want to talk about quickly when engaging in a meaningful, real-life situation. In addition, it allows for speaking to be possibly integrated with the writing skill. It requires little preparation and takes about 15–20 minutes to execute.

Procedure

1. Hand out cards or sheets of paper and have your students each write down (a) one learning strategy that they have found helpful in learning Arabic and why and (b) one challenging aspect of learning the language and why (in 5 minutes).
2. Ask each student to find a partner with whom to discuss and share their learning strategy and challenging aspect of learning the language in no more than 3 minutes.
3. Once done, ask each student to find a new partner to discuss and share with them the same in no more than 3 minutes.
4. Repeat the process one more time so that each student has paired with three different groups.
5. Call on some volunteers to share what they have learned from their partners.

Variations

a. As a follow-up, redivide your students into groups and have them write a composition on five challenging aspects of learning Arabic and five learning strategies to best overcome them (in 10 minutes).
b. Collect the assignments for feedback and corrections later.
c. Alternatively, the composition can be assigned individually as an assignment outside of class.

19. *What is the truth?* ما الحقيقة؟

Purpose

To provide learners with practice speaking and develop some analytical abilities when speaking. It requires no preparation and takes about 15 minutes to execute. It allows for the integration of speaking with the listening skill, as it requires listening carefully to the choices and subsequent focused interaction on what is true and what is false.

Procedure

1. Ask your students to take 2–3 minutes and write down four statements about anything, one of which is true and the rest are false.
2. Divide your students into dyads and have each student share their statements with their partner.
3. Each partner has up to 4 minutes to ask questions (1 minute per statement) to help them determine the true statement.
4. Allow one additional minute for the partner to decide which statement is the true one.
5. The partner takes their turn in sharing their four statements and follows the same steps.
6. Rotate among the groups and note down errors you may overhear your students making.
7. Upon concluding the activity, go over the errors and discuss them as a whole class.

Variations

a. Instead of pair work, implement the technique as a whole-class activity.
b. Have the student with the statements face their classmates and either share the statements verbally or on the board (or via a document projector).
c. Have other classmates take turns (in a chain fashion) asking questions about the statements for up to 4 minutes.
d. Allow your students to vote on the true statement.

(See also Bolen 2015.)

20.   تكلّموا أسرَع فأسرَع 120/90/60 or 4/3/2

Purpose

To provide learners with practice to improve their fluency in speaking. By reducing speech time each time they speak on the same topic, it trains learners to eliminate or reduce their speech pauses and use more than one style and structure for their sentences by attempting to reformulate their sentences to be shorter. It may be challenging to implement the first time, but learners will get used to it later. It requires little to no preparation and takes about 15 minutes to execute. It allows for the integration of speaking with listening, as it requires a listener in all its three stages.

Procedure

1. Come up with a set of well-known topics with which your students are familiar and at their level.

54   Speaking techniques

2. Allow your students 3–5 minutes for each to prepare to talk about any of the designated topics in no more than 120 seconds (i.e., 2 minutes).
3. Allow your students to take notes containing key words but not sentences.
4. Divide your students into dyads and have each student talk about their topic to their partner in no more than 120 seconds.
5. Redivide your students into different dyads (so that each student will have a different partner in a new group) and have each student talk about their topic to their partner in no more than 90 seconds.
6. Divide your students a third time into different dyads (so that each student will have a different partner in a new group) and have each student talk about their topic to their partner in no more than 60 seconds.
7. In the second and third stages, your students should talk about the same information they did in the first stage.
8. Rotate among the groups and note down errors you may hear your students making.
9. Upon concluding the activity, go over the errors and correct them as a whole class.

Variations

a. Instead of the stages over 120, 90, and 60 seconds, allow for the transition along the three stages to be 4 minutes, then 3 minutes, and then 2 minutes; this allows students more time for each stage.
b. For students whose proficiency level is at the intermediate middle, allow them to take notes comprising sentences and allow them to revise their notes each time they work with a new group,

(See also Nation 2009; Yang 2014.)

3.   Developing speaking at the advanced level

At the advanced level, speaking involves communication at the paragraph and extended discourse levels and ranges from the use of high-frequency vocabulary and structures to the use of low-frequency (and specialized) vocabulary and (more complex) structures. At this stage, for pedagogical reasons and to reflect real life situations, it is expected to implement techniques that integrate speaking with one or more skills in addition to those that focus on speaking as an isolated skill. While using a form or function through a skill, learners can activate it or recycle it through another and achieve control and automaticity through others. In addition to the techniques that follow, some of the techniques in the intermediate section can be used for the advanced level when the texts and topics used are suitable for the advanced level.

Speaking techniques 55

21. *Picture-based story* قصص مصوّرة

Purpose

To provide learners with practice speaking at the paragraph level. It allows for the integration of speaking with possibly the writing skill, as it requires learners to write a story before presenting it. It requires little preparation and takes about 20 minutes to execute.

Procedure

1. Prepare three pictures: the first one about a person, the second contains objects related to the person, and the third contains additional objects or things related to the person.
2. Divide your students into dyads, hand them out the first picture, and have each group create a background story about the person (such as who this person is and how they might relate to him) in 4 minutes; students can take down notes.
3. Hand out the second picture to the groups to have them create a story about the person (the objects in the pictures can relate to the person in positive or negative ways) in 4 minutes.
4. Hand out the third picture to the groups to have them complete the story about the person (the objects in the pictures can relate to the person in positive or negative ways) in 4 minutes.
5. Remind your students to use connectors to connect the sentences and parts of the story (the background, story, conclusion).
6. Redivide your students into groups of 4 comprising one member of the previous groups and have each group member tell their previous group's version of the story to the group in no more than 2 minutes so that it will take the group 8 minutes.

Variations

a. At the end of the activity, the dyads can be reconstituted to write down their story and fine-tune it if necessary (in about 7–10 minutes).
b. The written stories can be collected by the teacher for written feedback and corrections later.

(See also Sepulveda 2012.)

22. *News reports* تقديمات عن مقتطفات إخبارية

Purpose

To provide learners with practice speaking at the paragraph level. It allows for the integration of speaking with listening or reading, and possibly writing, as it

56 Speaking techniques

requires learners to listen to or read the news or source of current issues and write a summary before presenting it in class. It requires no preparation and takes about 15 minutes to execute.

Procedure

1. Assign your students to report on a piece of news or a current (social or political) issue.
2. Ask your students to limit the homework assignment to certain topics of your choice (depending on student needs in class), such as politics, business, communication, transportation, science, and so on.
3. Have each student stand in front of the class to present the information they had worked on in no more than 2–3 minutes; the information presented should include the author's name, the news organization, and information that answers what, who, when, where, how, and why.
4. The student should not read (but can glance at notes) and should be prepared to answer questions from the class on the content of the presentation.

Variations

a. Before they present their news reports, divide your students into dyads to rehearse their presentations in 5 minutes.
b. Other topics include reports about a book/article your students have read or a film they have watched.
c. The written summary reports can be collected for correction and grading as written composition assignments.

23. Group trip رحلة جماعية

Purpose

To provide learners with practice speaking and allow for improving on fluency at the extended discourse level of discussing pros and cons or advantages and disadvantages. The technique allows for the integration of speaking with possibly the writing skill. It takes little preparation and takes about 20–30 minutes to execute, depending on the number of students in class.

Procedure

1. Prepare a list of 3–5 possible destinations on index cards or sheets of paper, such as vacation resorts, tourist sites, historical sites, national monuments, foreign cities, summer-abroad programs, and so on.
2. Distribute a card to each student and divide your students into groups of 2–4.

Speaking techniques   57

3. Ask each group to discuss and decide on their selection of one destination based on a collective decision, taking into account the pros and cons of the listed destinations, in 8–10 minutes.
4. Through a reporter delegated by the group, each group reports on their selection and the pros and cons that they considered in their decision.
5. Other students in the class can ask questions or comment on the pros and cons considered.

Variations

a. Instead of choosing one single destination, ask each group to rank order the listed destination according to the group members' preferences.
b. In addition to considering the pros and cons or advantages and disadvantages, each group can take other reasons into consideration such as how group members will spend their time there.
c. Upon concluding the activity, and if time permits, ask each group to write three short paragraphs: one in which they describe the advantages of the destinations, another in which they describe the disadvantages of the destination, and a third in which they describe their final decision and why.
d. Collect the written paragraphs for feedback and corrections later.
e. Alternatively, the written part can be assigned as a homework assignment outside of the class.

24. *Optimists and pessimists* متشائمون ومتفائلون

Purpose

To provide learners with practice speaking and promote fluency at the extended discourse level of defending an opinion with different arguments. The technique allows for the integration of speaking with possibly the writing skill. It requires little to no preparation and takes about 20–30 minutes to execute, depending on the number of students in class.

Procedure

1. Prepare a topic on an issue that people may have two opposite perspectives, such as الرياضة "sport," التكنولوجيا "technology," وسائل التواصل الاجتماعي "social media," and السكن في المدينة "living in the city," among others.
2. Divide the class into two groups: an optimistic group adopting a positive attitude towards the topic and a pessimistic group adopting a negative attitude.
3. Elicit an optimistic statement from the optimist group on the topic such as "sport is good for one's health."

58   Speaking techniques

4. Elicit an opposite response from the pessimist group such as "some sports are harmful to one's health."
5. Repeat the process back and forth and have them provide reasons for their statements until the two groups have exhausted all their statements and arguments and all the students in each group have participated.
6. Discuss with the class if either of the two groups was more convincing and why.
7. Offer feedback and corrections on any patterns of errors students have made.

Variations

a. Upon concluding the activity, redivide your students into groups of dyads (one from the optimist group and one from the pessimist group) and have them write two paragraphs one on each attitude by couching the two attitudes in terms of the advantages and disadvantages or pros and cons of the topic discussed (in 10 minutes).
b. Limit the advantages and disadvantages to three arguments each.
c. Remind your students to use connecters so that their sentences and paragraphs are coherent and connected.
d. Collect the written responses for feedback and corrections later.

25. *Debating* إجراء مناظرة

Purpose

To provide learners with practice speaking at the extended discourse level of defending an opinion with multiple arguments. The technique allows for the integration of speaking with reading and writing, as it requires learners to research the topic and read about it and then write down groups' specific arguments. It requires no preparation and takes about 20–30 minutes to execute, depending on the number of students in class.

Procedure

1. Assign a debate assignment on a current, controversial topic such as الهجرة "immigration" and ask your students to prepare six arguments for a subsequent class.
2. Divide your students into groups of 3 to work on the assignment as follows: two as the researchers and one as the presenter.
3. On the due date of the assignment, allow each presenter to present the group's arguments (in 6 minutes).
4. Following the presentation of arguments of a group, open the floor for discussion, where students in the class can ask questions and any of the group members (i.e., the presenter or researchers) can answer.

Speaking techniques 59

Variations

a. To provide students with practice to improvise their response to the function of defending an opinion, allow for the entire activity to be conducted in class.
b. Divide the class into groups of 3, all of whom will be presenters.
c. Assign groups to either in favor or against stance with respect to the controversial topic.
d. Ask each group member to come up with one argument for or against, depending on their group membership.
e. Have two sets of groups (one for and one against) at a time to debate the topic in front of the class.
f. Following the presentations of the arguments by the two groups, open the floor for discussion in which students in the class can ask questions pertaining to either stance and members of a group respond to the questions, depending on their stance.
g. Alternatively, allow group members of the opposing stance to ask the other group questions that will challenge the latter's stance.

Chapter 3

Reading techniques

1. Developing reading at the novice level

It is widely acknowledged that a number of subskills are involved in reading in general, whether in first- or second-language reading. However, the focus here is on developing reading fluency and reading comprehension skills, along with implementing bottom-up (by decoding the text at the word and sentence level) and top-down (by activating background knowledge and conceptual schemata) processing as well as strategies of figuring out the meanings of words from the context as well as roots and patterns. At the novice level, reading encompasses the ability to recognize written Arabic at the letter, morpheme, word, memorized chunks, and phrase levels and toward the novice high (to pitch it a little higher than ACTFL guidelines) at the sentence and simple text levels of basic everyday life topics. For the development of reading fluency at the letter, morpheme, word, memorized chunks, and phrase levels, most techniques included in the listening section of the novice level can be used here as well. These are not included here to avoid repetition. A reading technique is usually implemented as a pre-reading, during-reading, post-reading activity, or all these combined.

1. Spot the words البحث عن الكلمات

Purpose

To provide learners with practice recognizing familiar words in texts which they have already studied or in novel texts at the same level. It requires little to no preparation and takes about 5–10 minutes to execute.

Procedure

1. Find a simple text that contains words with which your students are familiar or preselect a text from your students' textbook that they have covered in class or have not but remain within their level.
2. Preselect such words or phrases and ask your students to spot them in the text by underlining or drawing a circle around them after you read them.

Reading techniques 61

3. If the text consists of more than one paragraph, identify the paragraph to make it easy for them to spot the words.
4. Go over your students' responses in class along with the phrases and sentences with which they occur and have your students read them.

Variations

a. Check if your students know the meanings of the words by asking them to write their meanings in English, their synonyms, or their antonyms.
b. Reward students who spot words the soonest.

2. *Sorting out words into lists* تصنيف الكلمات في قوائم

Purpose

To provide learners with practice recognizing familiar words and sorting them into their superordinate categories. It requires little preparation and takes about 5–10 minutes to execute.

Procedure

1. Prepare a list of 10 words belonging to two categories (such as food and clothing) either typed on a handout or written on the board (or displayed on a screen or via a document projector) in random order.
2. Ask your students to group the words under two categories: مأكولات "food" and ملابس "clothing" (in 4–5 minutes).
3. Go over 2–3 samples of students' lists by having students read their lists.
4. Allow other students to provide corrections.

Variations

a. To make the activity a little more challenging, increase the number of words to be sorted out to 15–20 words.
b. Ask your students to label the categories to which the words belong.
c. Modify the activity so that instead of grouping words together, students are required to tell the odd member out (i.e., by flagging out the word or words that do not belong to the words).

3. *"Bingo"* سباق "البنغو"

Purpose

To provide learners with practice recognizing familiar words in texts that they have studied. It requires little to no preparation and takes about 5 minutes to execute.

62 Reading techniques

Procedure

1. Write on the board (or display on a screen or via a document projector) a list of 15–20 words that occurred in a recent text or texts covered in class.
2. Ask your students to write down six words that they recognize and know their meanings.
3. Read aloud six words that you have predetermined with short pauses between them.
4. When a student hears a word that they had written down, they should cross it out and once they cross out all six words, the student must say "bingo."
5. Reward students who cross out all six words the soonest.

Variations

a. Identify a text or 2 and have your students spot six of the words you listed on the board.
b. Reward the one who spots six words the soonest.

(See also Ur and Wright 1992.)

4. Role-play تمثيل أدوار

Purpose

To provide learners with practice to develop their reading comprehension and recognize words from texts and contexts. It allows for the integration between reading comprehension and the speaking skill. It requires little preparation and takes about 10–15 minutes to execute.

Procedure

1. Find (through searching online) a level-appropriate text, such as a restaurant menu of Arabic food, preferably with pictures next to items and with three main sections including مُقَبِّلات "appetizers," أطباق "entrees," and مشروبات "drinks" (other appropriate texts can be flight schedules, weather forecast lists, catalog price lists, etc.).
2. Divide your students into groups of 2–5, acting as clients in a restaurant.
3. Assign yourself the role of the waiter.
4. Go around and distribute copies of the menu to students in each group (after greeting them) and offer them to look at the menu for a couple of minutes before ordering.
5. In the meantime, move to another group to do the same and so on.
6. Return to the first group and elicit from each group member what they would like to order from each of the three sections of the menu مُقَبِّلات "appetizers," أطباق "entrees," and مشروبات "drinks" just as a waiter normally does.

Reading techniques 63

7. Continue on and repeat the process with each group until each student has placed their order from the menu.
8. Provide definitions or explanations of items on the menu if necessary.

Variations

a. A student or several students can be assigned the role of waiters instead of the teacher.
b. Repeat the activity each time with a restaurant menu of food from a different region in the Arab world.
c. For role-play involving students recognizing and telling flight times and destinations, divide your students into clients and travel agents or travelers reading flight schedules and asking each other.

5. *Repeated reading aloud* القراءة الجهريّة مع التّكرار

Purpose

To provide learners with practice to develop reading fluency, as it raises their awareness of how words are connected at the phrase and sentence level together with following the rules for reading in Arabic. It also builds self-confidence, especially in more timid learners. It allows for the integration of reading with speaking, as it focuses on pronunciation. It requires little to no preparation and takes about 5 minutes to execute.

Procedure

1. Upon completing a given lesson or unit in the textbook, prepare typed copies of a text (e.g., of a dialogue or monologue) if a reading text is not available within the lesson.
2. Modify the text slightly so that the sentences are not too long and all internal short-vowel diacritics are placed, such as the following:

> اِسْمي أَحْمَد الشّامي. أَنا أَمْريكيّ مِنْ أَصْل سوريّ. أَسْكُن في مَدينة ديترويت في وِلاية ميشيغان. أَدْرُس اللُّغة العَرَبيّة في جامِعة في وِلاية ميشيغان أَيْضاً. والِدي أُسْتاذ في نَفْس الجامِعة. ووالِدَتي طَبيبة تَعْمَل في مَدينة ديربورن.

3. Ask your students to repeat after you in unison (i.e., as a whole class).
4. Start by reading at the phrase or chunk level one phrase/chunk at a time and your students repeat after you.
5. Read and have your students repeat each phrase/chunk 1–3 times as needed, depending on how well you hear your student are imitating you and pronouncing words correctly.

64 Reading techniques

6. You can exaggerate your pronunciation the first 1–2 time you read but adjust your reading to be normal in pronunciation and pace in the third time.
7. Do not move to the next phrase/chunk until you hear your students have imitated you well or reasonably well.
8. You may need to read and have your students repeat certain words in isolation if you hear them struggling with such words.
9. Once you have covered all the phrases/chunks of a sentence, read the whole sentence all at once 1–3 times and have your students repeat after you the whole sentence.
10. Repeat the same steps when you move to the second sentence and so on.
11. After you have completed reading the whole text, following the preceding procedure, tell your students you will now read the text one more time (and they will repeat after you) at the sentence level, but you will read only once and, therefore, encourage them to do their best.
12. Have each student read one sentence, the next student the next sentence, and so on until every student has read a sentence (you may need to repeat the text more than once so that all students have read) and provide correction when needed to each student misreading or mispronouncing any word or chunk.

Variations

a. Implement the same activity upon the completion of every lesson in the textbook.
b. Read and have your students repeat the texts of the previous lessons (one lesson at a time sequentially either in ascending or descending order) before or after reading and repeating the current text, but read the previous texts only once and do so at the sentence level.
c. Allow your students to audio record the activity, if they wish, so they can practice and work on their pronunciation and fluency outside of the classroom.

6. *Fast reading* القراءة السريعة

Purpose

To provide learners with practice to develop reading fluency, as it requires the repetition of the reading of a text with speed as a main factor and builds self-confidence in them. It also allows some focus on pronunciation. It requires little to no preparation and takes about 20 minutes to execute.

Procedure

1. Find a text such as the one in the previous activity from your students' textbook upon completing the lesson/unit.
2. Divide your students into two groups: readers and listeners.
3. Divide your students into dyads consisting of a reader and a listener.

Reading techniques 65

4. Have the readers read the text to their listening partners in 4 minutes (by timing them, saying ابدؤوا "Go" at the beginning and توقفوا "stop" at the end) and mark where each stopped (and urge readers not to compromise pronunciation and intelligibility).
5. Redivide your students into different dyads where readers have different listeners and have readers read the text in 3 minutes, following the same procedure (and urge readers not to compromise pronunciation and intelligibility).
6. Redivide your students into different dyads again where readers have different listeners (than the two previous dyads) and have readers read the text in 2 minutes, following the same procedure (and urge readers not to compromise pronunciation and intelligibility).
7. Readers can see now where they each time stopped and are expected to show improvement in reading speed.
8. Have your students exchange roles so that previous readers are now listeners and previous listeners are now readers.
9. Repeat the preceding process so that readers read the text to different listening partners in three steps: in 4 minutes, then in 3 minutes, and then in 2 minutes.

Variations

a. Provide an accuracy measure such as by rewarding the reader who makes the fewest errors in pronunciation and intelligibility in general.
b. A new level-appropriate text (containing previously known vocabulary and structures) can also be used, which will make the activity more interesting, and students can also develop their reading comprehension by attending to meaning.

(See also Nation 2009.)

7. *Sentence simplification* تسهيل الجمل

Purpose

To provide learners with practice to develop reading comprehension and proper sentence processing by breaking up long or nested sentences that may otherwise be confusing to them or may not enable them to get the full meaning. It requires little to no preparation and takes about 15–20 minutes to execute.

Procedure

1. Find a level-appropriate text of a short paragraph or select one from your students' textbook.
2. Have your students work individually or in groups of dyads to unpack the sentences into short ones (whether they are verbal or verbless) by placing a line at the end of each sentence (in 10 minutes) as in the following sample:

66 Reading techniques

> أُحِبّ بَيْتي كثيراً/لأنّه كَبير/ولَهُ حَديقة كَبيرة/لكِنّي لا أُحِبّ مَدينتي/لأنَّ الطَّقْس بارد دائماً في الشِّتاء//ودَرَجة الرُّطُوبة عالِية في الصَّيْف /. هذِهِ المَدينة صَغيرة جِدّاً /لِيْسَ فيها حَدائق عامّة كَثيرة/. لي صَديق واحِد فَقَط/اِسْمُه عادل /وهو طالِب في نَفْس الجامِعة/ يَدْرُس فيها التاريخ/.

3. Go over your students' responses by having each student read a sentence.

Variations

a. Repeat this technique often and from early on until your students are able to quickly identify the beginning and end of a sentence.
b. At a little later stage, develop this reading technique into a grammar technique in which students receive practice to distinguish between verbal and verbless sentences, identify the subject and object of the verb (in the verbal sentence), and identify the subject and predicate (in the verbless sentence; see the section of grammar techniques).
c. If grammatical (case and mood) endings are taught from early on, teach such endings as part of the explanation of the verbal and verbless sentence.

(See also Nation 2009.)

8. *Guessing then confirming* التخمين ثم التأكّد

Purpose

To provide learners with practice to develop reading fluency and reading comprehension as well as to develop top-down and bottom-up processing strategies of reading. It requires little to no preparation and takes about 15–20 minutes to execute, depending on the length of the text.

Procedure

1. Find a level-appropriate text of one short paragraph or select one from your students' textbook.
2. Read the text aloud once.
3. Have your students follow with their eyes as you read and ask them to try to understand the text as much as they can by relying on words they know and skipping words they do not know or recognize.
4. Elicit short responses from your students about what they understood from the text.
5. Have them read the text individually to themselves and ask them to underline five words that they do not know or recognize and would like you to explain.
6. Write the words on the board and go over them as a whole class, providing their meanings, synonyms, or antonyms.

Reading techniques **67**

7. Have them read the text a third time individually.
8. Elicit short responses from your students about what they understood from the text.

Variations

a. Have a student who can read well read the text aloud instead of you.
b. Instead of having your students read the text individually, divide the class into dyads and have them read the text to each other.

(See also Clark 1980.)

9. True/false comprehension questions صواب أم خطأ

Purpose

To provide learners with practice to read for meaning and develop their reading comprehension ability at the global level of getting the main ideas of a reading text. This can be in the form of short statements about the reading text whether they are true or false about general facts or the main ideas of a text. It requires little preparation and is executed as a post-reading activity. It takes about 20–30 minutes to execute.

Procedure

1. Upon reading a level-appropriate text (such as the text in the first activity above), provide your students with a sheet of paper with a blank column numbered according to the reading comprehension questions, each row containing a box for the true response and another for the false response to be checked when appropriate.
2. To make students focus on meaning, and not just guess the answers from the sequence of information in the text, change the order of some of the questions.
3. Divide your students into dyads and have them discuss and check the appropriate box based on their understanding of the text.
4. Go over your students' responses as a whole class.

Sample 1: **Students' Responses**   **True/False Statements**   ←

☑	خَطأ	☐	صَواب	1.	1. هو سوريّ
☑	خَطأ	☐	صَواب	2.	2. لا يَدْرُس اللُّغة العَرَبيّة
☐	خَطأ	☑	صَواب	3.	3. والِدَتُهُ طَبيبة.
☐	خَطأ	☑	صَواب	4.	4. والِدُهُ أُسْتاذ.
☑	خَطأ	☐	صَواب	5.	5. والِدَتُهُ تَعْمَل في الجامِعة.

68   Reading techniques

Variation

The format of the questions can alternatively be given as yes/no comprehension questions as in Sample 2.

Sample 2:   **Students' Responses**   **Yes/No questions on Text**   ←

1.   ☑ لا   ☐ نَعَم   .1   هَلْ هو سوريّ؟   .1

2.   ☐ لا   ☑ نَعَم   .2   هَلْ يَدْرُس اللُّغة العَرَبيّة؟   .2

3.   ☐ لا   ☑ نَعَم   .3   هَلْ والِدَتُهُ طَبيبة؟   .3

4.   ☐ لا   ☑ نَعَم   .4   هَلْ والِدُهُ أُسْتاذ؟   .4

5.   ☑ لا   ☐ نَعَم   .5   هَلْ والِدَتُهُ تَعْمَل في الجامِعة؟   .5

10. Rearranging scrambled sentences إعادة ترتيب الجمل المبعثرة

Purpose

To provide learners with practice to develop their reading fluency at the sentence level and attend to the meaning and relationships among ideas or statements in a text. It requires little preparation and takes about 10 minutes to execute.

Procedure

1. Find a level-appropriate text of a short paragraph or select one from your students' textbook that you have recently covered.
2. Type the sentences occurring in the text, placing them scrambled randomly one sentence on a separate line, as illustrated in the following scrambled sentences of a text:

> أ. أَسْكُن في مَدينة ديترويت في وِلاية ميشيغان.
> ب. اِسْمي أَحْمَد الشّامي.
> ج. أدْرُس اللُّغة العَرَبيّة في جامِعة في وِلاية ميشيغان أَيْضاً.
> د. أنا أمْريكيّ مِنْ أَصْل سوريّ.
> هـ. ووالِدَتي طَبيبة تَعْمَل في مَدينة ديربورن.
> و. والِدي أُسْتاذ في نَفْس الجامِعة.

3. Ask your students to read the sentences and arrange them into a coherent paragraph; no modification of any word is needed.

Reading techniques 69

4. Go over your students' responses as a whole class (e.g., by displaying a student's response via a document projector) and having a student read one sentence at a time and inviting class to confirm or disconfirm its right order.
5. Allow a different order of sentences if the order is appropriate.

Variations

a. Instead of rewriting the sentences, have your students number the sentences as they should occur in a paragraph by placing the number of each sentence to its right.
b. Divide your students into dyads and have them discuss and reorder the sentences in groups.

2. Developing reading at the intermediate level

At the intermediate level, reading is focused on simple texts about personal interests and familiar topics. At this stage, learners of Arabic will benefit greatly from continued reading practice in isolation. However, it may also be useful at times to implement techniques that integrate speaking with one or more skills as is done in the techniques that follow. A reading technique is usually implemented as a pre-reading, during-reading, post-reading activity, or all of these combined.

11. Getting the gist of the text المعلومات الرئيسة من النصّ استخراج

Purpose

To provide learners with practice to comprehend a reading text at the global level. Global comprehension questions usually relate to who, what, when, where, why, and how. A suitable text can be similar in size and content of news sub-headlines and similar clearly structured text (i.e., with no implied main idea of the text). It requires little preparation and takes about 20–25 minutes to execute.

Procedure

1. Find a level-appropriate text of interest or relevance to your students or use a text in their textbook which is clearly structured such as the following sample text.
2. Before reading the text, ask your students to process the text in terms of the six global comprehension question types: من "who," ما/ ماذا "what," متى "when," أين "where," لماذا "why," and كيف "how" such as the questions in the following text:

70 Reading techniques

Sample:

موعد إعلان نتيجة الثانوية العامة
قال وزير التربية والتعليم كريم السعيد إن نتيجة امتحانات الثانوية العامة لهذه السنة لن تظهر قبل شهرين من الآن أي قبل 20 أغسطس/آب الجاري، وربما تتأخر أكثر وذلك للتنسيق مع وزارة التعليم العالي من أجل تحديد علامات القبول في الجامعات في الاختصاصات المختلفة. وستعلن الوزارة عن النتائج عندئذ في المدارس الثانوية. وينتظر مئات الآلاف من الطلاب وأولياء الأمور بشوق ظهور نتيجة الثانوية العامة لهذا العام.

الأسئلة:

1. ما موضوع النصّ؟
2. مَن المُتَكَلِّم في النصّ؟
3. مَتى سَتَظهر نتائج الثانوية العامّة؟
4. أين سَتَظهر نتائج الثانوية العامّة؟
5. لِماذا لَنْ تظهر نتائج الثانوية العامّة اليوم؟
6. كيف ينتظر الطلاب نتائجهم؟

3. Have your students read the text individually (silently) once or twice or in groups of dyads, each reading the text to their partner once (in 5 minutes).
4. Prepare 5–6 global comprehension question types appropriate to the text and have your students answer the questions in pairs (in 5–7 minutes).
5. Go over the answers to the questions as a whole class, with each pair addressing one question (where one reads the question and the other answers it).
6. Have students from other groups validate the correct answers or provide corrections.

Variations

a. After your students get used to the format of this activity, have them come up with the global 5–6 set of questions in pairs (after having read the text).
b. Go over the formed question as a whole class.
c. Redistribute the groups of dyads so that each student will have a different partner from the previous group.

12. The comprehension race سباق الفهم

Purpose

To provide learners with practice to develop their reading comprehension by attending to meaning, in particular scanning texts for specific information, as a post-reading activity. It requires little preparation and livens up the classroom environment by

Reading techniques 71

having students move around. One possible disadvantage of this technique is that
because of getting involved in a race and moving around to answer comprehension
questions, it may be more suitable for young learners. It takes about 30 minutes to
execute.

Procedure

1. Find a level-appropriate text of interest or relevance to your students or use a
   text in their textbook.
2. Prepare comprehension questions in strips and place them randomly in a pile.
3. Divide your students into two or more competing teams.
4. Upon reading the text, a runner from each team runs to a pile, picks up a strip/
   question, and takes it to the team to find the answer.
5. Once the team finds the answer, the runner takes the answer to the teacher, picks
   up the next question from the pile, and so on.
6. Go over the questions and answers as a whole class.
7. Reward the team which has the most accurate answers.

Variations

a. Divide the strips/questions equally among the teams and ask them to begin discussing and answering the questions at the same time.
b. The team that answers all the questions the sooner determines the end of the race
   and is declared the winner if they have the most correct answers.

(See also Day and Park 2005.)

13. Guess the comprehension questions خمّنوا أسئلة الفهم

Purpose

To provide learners with practice to develop their reading comprehension by
attending to meaning and to promote bottom-up and top-down processing of the
text. It requires little preparation and takes about 35 minutes to execute.

Procedure

1. Find a level-appropriate text of interest or relevance to your students or use a
   text in their textbook.
2. Inform your students of the topic of the text.
3. Write a list of key words of the text on the board (or display them on a screen or
   via a document projector) and tell your students the words will be part of questions on the text.
4. Read the words aloud and have your students repeat after you chorally.
5. Go over words that your students do not recognize.

72   Reading techniques

6. Have your students read the text individually and ask them to guess and form the questions (based on the key words you provided) and provide answers to them in 15–20 minutes.
7. Go over your students' responses as a whole class whether they guessed the right questions and reveal the questions to them one by one (in 10 minutes).
8. Have your students ask each other the questions in a chain fashion.

Variations

a. Have your students work on the reading and the questions within groups of dyads.
b. Have dyads report to class first the questions they guessed and reward the groups that guessed most of the right questions or closest versions to them.
c. As a whole-class activity, have groups ask each other the questions and answer them in a chain fashion, 1 group asking the next one and so on.

(See also Nation 2009.)

14. *Guess the text* خمّنوا النصّ

Purpose

To provide learners with practice to develop their reading comprehension by attending to meaning and interacting creatively with meaning. It allows for the integration of reading comprehension with the writing and speaking skills. It requires little preparation and takes about 40 minutes to execute.

Procedure

1. Find a level-appropriate text of interest or relevance to your students or use a text in their textbook.
2. Write a list of key words of the text on the board (or display them on a screen or via a document projector) vertically and according to their occurrence in the text.
3. Read the words aloud and have your students repeat after you chorally.
4. Go over words that your students do not recognize.
5. Divide your students into dyads and have each group write a short paragraph, using the key words, guessing the meaning of the content of the text to be read (in about 10–15 minutes).
6. Have your students within their groups read the text and modify the guesses that they made about the text to match the factual content of the text (in about 10–15 minutes).
7. Go over 1–3 samples of your students' responses as a whole class, eliciting further modifications from the class to match the actual text content.

Reading techniques **73**

Variation

As a follow-up post-reading activity, if time permits, invite your students to ask language-related questions (i.e., vocabulary and grammar) that they may have about the text and/or any difficult part of the text they may have encountered. (See also Fisher et al. 2011.)

15. *Recap and discuss more* لخّصوا وتناقشوا أكثر

Purpose

To provide learners with practice to develop their reading comprehension by attending to meaning as a second layer of analysis of the text and zeroing in on its main as well as secondary ideas. It allows for the integration of reading comprehension with the speaking skill. It is mainly used as a post-reading activity and requires no preparation. It takes about 15–20 minutes to execute.

Procedure

1. Upon reading a text (from your students' textbook or from outside the book) and answering comprehension questions on it, elicit a summary of the text from the whole class (orally) by having each student contribute a part of it in a chain fashion (in 5–10 minutes).
2. Provide feedback by means of recasting your students' responses or inviting corrections from other students.
3. After your students provide a full summary of the text, invite them to ask any questions they have about the text or questions raised by the text, taking into account other aspects of the text; that is, those not included in the comprehension questions that they have already answered (in about 5–10 minutes).
4. Each student should ask the next student (or class) at least 1 question.

Variations

a. Have questions already prepared to ask your students to address other aspects of the texts not included in the comprehension questions and distribute 1 or 2 to each student so they can use them to ask.
b. As a final stage, invite your students to ask language-related questions (i.e., vocabulary and grammar) that they may have about the text.

(See also Fisher et al. 2011.)

16. *Reading fast* القراءة السريعة

Purpose

To provide learners with practice to develop their reading fluency and skimming ability to get a quick overview of the text. It also serves as a confidence booster and

74   Reading techniques

is mainly used as an activity during reading. It requires little to no preparation and takes about 15–20 minutes to execute.

Procedure

1. Inform your students of the topic of the text and provide them with any necessary background or contextual information helpful to understand the text.
2. Inform your students they will be engaged in a speed reading of the text and inform them of the activity's main reading rules including skipping words they do not know and not using any outside sources (e.g., their notes, their textbook, or a dictionary).
3. Distribute copies of the text to your students on the back side and ask them to watch your signal to start reading fast for 2 minutes and stop after that.
4. Instruct them to mark down where they have reached.
5. Elicit short responses from them about what they have read and understood (in 3–5 minutes).
6. Instruct them to complete reading the text.
7. Have them work on the comprehension questions using any post-reading technique.

Variations

a. Reward students who read more than others within the 2 minutes.
b. Repeat the process of having your students read fast at 2-minute intervals and elicit from them short responses about what they have read and understood after each time.

(See also Labmeier and Vockell 1971; Macalister 2010.)

17.   What is the advertisement for? عَمَّ الإعلان؟

Purpose

To provide learners with practice to develop their reading comprehension by attending to meeting. It requires some preparation in finding some advertisements that can be searched online. It allows for the integration of reading comprehension with the speaking skill and takes about 30–40 minutes to execute.

Procedure

1. Prepare a number of advertisements printed on paper on each of which the name of what is advertised is removed.
2. Divide your students into dyads and distribute an advertisement to each pair to discuss and identify what the advertisement is about and why in 8–10 minutes. If the dyad is uncertain, they can offer three possible matches.
3. Exchange two advertisements between two dyads to discuss and identify what the advertisement is about and why in 8–10 minutes.

Reading techniques **75**

4. Each dyad shows and discusses one advertisement with the class and offers the dyad's possible match or matches and why.
5. Other dyads who worked on the same advertisements are allowed to agree or disagree and present their reasons.
6. Other students in the class are also invited to share their views.

Variations

a. Depending on class time, allow the exchange of advertisements among dyads 2–3 times or more so that each time a dyad discusses a different advertisement, depending on the number of advertisements used.
b. Have your students find similar advertisements or make their own and bring them to class for a similar class activity.

18. *Information gap* نقص في المعلومات

Purpose

To provide learners with practice to develop their reading comprehension by attending to meeting. It requires little preparation in finding a level-appropriate text about a topic of interest or relevance to students. It allows for the integration of reading comprehension with the speaking skill and takes about 25–30 minutes to execute.

Procedure

1. Find a level-appropriate text on a topic of interest or relevance to your students and print multiple copies.
2. Remove some information from each copy. For example, if the text is about a trip, one copy contains all the information about the trip except the place; another copy contains all the information except the transportation method; one copy contains all the information except the date and so on.
3. Divide your students into groups according to the number of information gaps in the text. Thus, if the text contains three information gaps, divide your students into groups of 3.
4. Ask your students to read the text to each other and discuss it among themselves to find the missing information (in 15 minutes).
5. Go over the missing information in the text as a whole class.

Variations

a. As a follow-up, have your students come up with the best possible title of the text that represents the main idea of the text.

76 Reading techniques

b. Have your students first discuss the best possible title in different groups (of 3s) and why.
c. Have each group report to the class their best matching title and provide their reasons.

19. 3/2/1 لخّصوا وعبّروا واسألوا

Purpose

To provide learners with practice to develop their reading comprehension by attending to meaning with some focus on grammar and structure. It requires little preparation and takes about to 35 minutes to execute. It allows for the integration of reading comprehension with the speaking skill.

Procedure

1. Find a level-appropriate text on a topic of interest or relevance to your students and print multiple copies.
2. Ask your students to read the text individually and come up with three main ideas about the text, two sentences that they liked in the text, and one question they have about the text in about 15 minutes, depending on the length of the text or parts of the text on which you are working on one part at a time; distribute a handout of what is required in which they can fill out the information, along the following outline:

3 • الفكرة الأولى: . . . .
   • الفكرة الثانية: . . . .
   • الفكرة الثالثة: . . . .
2 • الجملة الأولى: . . . .
   • الجملة الثانية: . . . .
1 • السؤال: . . . .

3. Divide your students into groups of three and have them discuss the three main ideas of the text that each has come up with and have them refine or agree on the three main ideas of the text (in 7 minutes).
4. Discuss as a whole class or between groups the three main ideas of the text.
5. Redivide the class into dyads and have each group discuss the two sentences that each student liked and why (in 5 minutes).
6. Discuss as a whole class the sentences that your students liked.
7. Have your students ask each other (in a chain fashion) their questions about the text.

Reading techniques　77

Variations

a. Instead of discussing the main ideas as a whole class, redivide the class into two groups and have them come up each with a summary of the text not to exceed 25 words.
b. Go over the two summaries in class.

(See also Faber 2015.)

20. Come up with the questions or summarize the text
ضعوا أسئلة الفهم أو لخِّصوا النصّ

Purpose

To provide learners with practice to develop their reading comprehension by attending to meaning. It allows the integration of reading comprehension with the speaking skill. It requires little preparation and takes about 30–40 minutes to execute, depending on the length of the text.

Procedure

1. Find a level-appropriate text on a topic of interest or relevance to your students (1–2 paragraphs) or use a text in their textbook.
2. Divide your students into groups of dyads.
3. Have half the groups read and discuss the text and come up with a summary of the main ideas of the text (in 15 minutes).
4. Have the other half of the groups read and discuss the text and come up with comprehension questions (4–5 questions) about what they have read (in 15 minutes).
5. Have the summary dyads each report their summary to the class (in 10 minutes).
6. Have the questions dyads ask the summary dyads their comprehension questions about the text (in 10 minutes).

Variations

a. If the text consists of more than one paragraph, follow the procedure one paragraph at a time.
b. Allow for some scaffolding for the summarizing groups (by asking them to come up with 3–5 statements limited to 25 words) and the questions groups (by providing them with key words of the text on which they should base their questions).

78   Reading techniques

3.   Developing reading at the advanced level

At the advanced level, reading is focused on the paragraph and extended discourse levels about general and professional topics that are familiar or unfamiliar. At this stage, for pedagogical reasons and to reflect real-life situations, it is expected to implement techniques that integrate reading with one or more skills in addition to those which focus on reading as an isolated skill. While using a form or function through one skill, learners can activate it or recycle it through another and achieve control and automaticity through others. In addition to the techniques included here, some of the techniques in the intermediate section can be used for the advanced level when the texts and topics used are suitable for the advanced level. A reading technique is usually implemented as a pre-reading, during-reading, post-reading activity, or all of these combined.

21.   Summarize in your own way لخّصوا بأسلوبكم الخاصّ

Purpose

To provide learners with practice to primarily develop their reading comprehension by attending to meaning, as learners are required to provide a summary of their understanding of a text (narrative or expository), in particular their ability to gist texts by identifying main ideas and key concepts of a text and its most important parts. It allows for the integration of reading comprehension with the writing skill (and possibly the speaking skill) so that learners can receive feedback on their comprehension as well as writing. The technique mimics real-life situations in which we often need to know the gist of what we read. It requires little to no preparation and, depending on the length of the text, takes about 30–45 minutes to execute.

Procedure

1. Find a level-appropriate text on a topic of interest or relevance to your students or use a text in their textbook of 3–5 paragraphs.
2. Divide your students into dyads and ask them to read the text to each other, paying extra attention to the title, headings, beginning, middle, and end of the text.
3. Limit the number of sentences or words that your students can use in summarizing the text (e.g., three sentences per paragraph not to exceed 25 words).
4. Ask your students to come up with a title or heading for each paragraph if there are no such headings.
5. Ask your students to combine the sentences to write up a short summary and eliminate any redundant words after incorporating the headings into the sentences.
6. Go over 1–2 sample summaries (depending on time available) as a whole class, displaying them to class (e.g., via a document projector) and inviting more refined suggestions and corrections.
7. Collect all summaries to provide feedback on factual and writing accuracy later outside of class.

Variations

a. Preassign the text to be read outside of the classroom before class so that students will take less time reading the text and the activity will mainly be a post-reading activity.
b. Have the groups of dyads exchange their summaries so that each group will attempt to provide feedback and corrections to both factual and writing accuracy of the paragraph of another group.
c. Have your students incorporate the feedback and collect the summaries to provide feedback later.

22. *Retell a summary of the text* تبادلوا ملخصاتكم للنصّ

Purpose

To provide learners with practice to primarily develop their reading comprehension by attending to meaning, as learners are required to provide a summary of their understanding of a text (narrative or expository), in particular their ability to gist texts by identifying main ideas and key concepts of a text. It allows for the integration of reading comprehension with the speaking skill (and possibly the writing skill) so that learners need to retell a summary of the text. The technique mimics real-life situations in which we often need to know the gist of what we read. It requires some preparation and, depending on the length of the text, takes about 30–45 minutes to execute.

Procedure

1. Find a level-appropriate text on a topic of interest or relevance to your students or use a text in their textbook of 3–5 paragraphs.
2. Divide your students into dyads and divide the texts into 3–5 parts, depending on the number of paragraphs.
3. Assign different students to read different parts or paragraphs of the text and encourage them to take (2–3) notes about the main ideas and most important information (in 10–15 minutes) and instruct them they will need to report a summary of what they have read to other students in class.
4. Divide your students who have read the same parts or paragraphs to discuss what they have read and compare their notes (in 10 minutes).
5. Redivide your students into new dyads pairing students who read different parts or paragraphs of the text and have each student report the summary to their partner (in 10 minutes).
6. Redivide your students into different dyads so students can continue to report their summaries to new partners.
7. Rotate between groups to ensure your students are reporting actual summaries, not just random comments or disconnected statements.

80 Reading techniques

Variations

a. Preassign the text to be read outside of the classroom before class so that students will take less time reading the text and the activity will mainly be a post-reading activity.
b. After your students report their summaries to their partners within dyads, redivide students into larger groups so that each group comprises one student of each of the first dyads so that one student is responsible for a summary/part of the text. Have your students collaborate to write a summary of the full text.
c. Collect the written summaries of the text to provide feedback later.

23. *Comparing texts* مقارنة بين النصوص

Purpose

To provide learners with practice to develop their reading comprehension by attending to meaning and reading texts critically by comparing different points of view. It allows for the integration of reading comprehension with the speaking skill. It requires some preparation and, depending on the length of the texts used, takes about 35–45 minutes to execute.

Procedure

1. Find (e.g., by searching online for) three texts of similar length on a similar topic such as a recent event in the news or a current issue (social, political, economic, etc.) of interest to your students. If the topic is related to an event reported in the news, choose the texts from three competing (Arabic) media platforms, such as Al Jazjeera, Al Arabiya, and the BBC.
2. Divide your students into groups of 3. Each group is given a different text and is asked to discuss the main ideas of the text in 10–15 minutes.
3. Redivide your students into groups of 3, consisting of students who read all three texts.
4. Have your students discuss the three texts, paying attention to three types of differences between the three texts: (a) in terms of content (i.e., at the level of details and whether some information is present in one text but not in the other two texts), (b) point of view (i.e., which one is likely biased or unbiased), and (c) style (which one is easiest to understand) and how (in 15 minutes).
5. Have three sample groups report to the class the outcomes of their discussion, each group reporting on one type of difference and their reasons, and allow other groups to agree or disagree by providing their reasons (in about 10–15 minutes).

Variations

a. Depending on the texts found and/or time constraints, focus can be exclusively on only one of the three differences: content, point of view, or style.

Reading techniques 81

b. Alternatively, the technique can be limited to two texts and students in this case can be divided into dyads.

(See also Watkins 2018.)

24. Relating background knowledge and personal experiences الربط بالمعرفة السابقة والخبرات الشخصية

Purpose

To provide learners with practice to develop their reading comprehension by attending to meaning and relating the reading to their background knowledge and personal experiences. It allows for the integration of reading comprehension with the speaking skill. It requires little preparation and, depending on the length of the texts used, takes about 40–45 minutes to execute. The technique fits as a pre-reading, during-reading, and post-reading activity.

Procedure

1. Find a level-appropriate text of 3–5 paragraphs (on a topic of a recent event, an issue of common interest, or an issue that can be conveyed from different perspectives) or use a text in your students' textbook.
2. Prior to reading the text, introduce the topic of the text to your students.
3. Elicit (in a chain fashion) 1–2 responses from each student of "what they already know about the topic" ماذا يعرفون عن الموضوع
4. Elicit (in a chain fashion) 1–2 responses from each student of "what they would like to know about the topic" ماذا يحبون أن يعرفوا عن الموضوع
5. Divide your students into dyads and have them read and discuss the text (in 20 minutes) and have them each agree to 3–5 statements of what they have learned about the topic.
6. Have each group report to the class what they have learned.
7. Have each student (in a chain fashion) relate some information in the text to their own personal experiences or life or those whom they know.

Variations

a. In the pre-reading stage, have each student write down 4–5 statements of what they already know about the topic and 4–5 statements of what they would like to know about it.
b. During the reading stage, have each student write 4–5 statements of what they learned from the text.
c. In the post-reading stage, divide your students into dyads to discuss with their partner how some of information of the text relates to their personal experiences or lives.

82 Reading techniques

d. Transition the activity into a writing activity assignment (outside of class) to combine the statements they wrote into a composition describing the topic, what they know about it, and how some of its content relates to their personal experiences.

(See also Watkins 2018.)

25. I agree and do not agree أَتَفق ولا أَتَفق

Purpose

To provide learners with practice to develop their reading comprehension by attending to meaning, reading texts critically, and exploring ways to support an opinion on a controversial issue or an issue of general interest. It allows for the integration of reading comprehension with speaking and (possibly) writing skills. It requires little preparation and, depending on the length of the texts used, takes about 40–45 minutes to execute. The technique fits as a pre-reading, during-reading, and post-reading activity.

Procedure

1. Find a level-appropriate text or use a text in your students' textbook of 3–5 paragraphs on a topic such as الرياضة الاحترافية "professional sport," التكنولوجيا "technology," وسائل التواصل الاجتماعية "social media," البيئة "the environment," and so on.
2. Prior to reading the text, introduce the topic of the text to your students.
3. Using their background knowledge and personal experience on the topic, have each student complete three stem statements starting with: أَتَفق "I agree" and three stem statements, starting with لا أَتَفق "I do not agree" (in 5–7 minutes) in relation to the topic.
5. Divide your students into dyads and have them read and discuss the text (in 20–25 minutes).
6. Ask each student to revise or confirm their six statements based on their reading of the text and the perspectives of the text, providing reasons.
7. Have each student express to the class three statements expressing agreement with the perspective of the text and three opposing ones and provide reasons.

Variations

a. Depending on the level of your students, provide some scaffolding by making stem sentences (in a handout) that are more detailed, along with the following, if the topic is on professional sport: أتفق مع كاتب النصّ أنّ . . . "I agree with the writer of the text that . . ." and لا أتفق مع كاتب النصّ أنّ . . ." "I do not agree with the writer of the text that . . ."

Reading techniques 83

b. Instead of the "I agree" and "I do not agree" statements, ask students to list 3 محاسن "advantages" and 3 مساوئ disadvantages of the topic, providing reasons briefly.

c. Transition the activity into a writing activity where students (in groups) are asked to write 2 paragraphs on the topic by incorporating their statements and providing reasons.

d. Collect your students' writings for feedback later.

(See also Faber 2015.)

Chapter 4

Writing techniques

1. Developing writing at the novice level

Writing is viewed here in terms of the ability to produce written language to meet functional needs at the word, phrase, and memorized chunk levels. At the novice high level, speaking is also pitched (a little higher than the ACTFL guidelines) at the sentence level. At higher subsequent levels, it involves production at the sentence, paragraph, and then extended discourse levels and ranges from the use of high-frequency vocabulary and structures to the use of low-frequency (and specialized) vocabulary and (more complex) structures (along ACTFL's proficiency guidelines, 2012). With the implementation of the various techniques along the proficiency scale, the development of the writing skill takes into account writing fluency, complexity, and accuracy (of spelling, word choice, and grammar) of the learner's production and is one that is viewed (beyond the early stages) as a process rather than a product. To simplify things, a writing technique can be implemented as a pre-drafting, during-drafting, post-drafting activity, or all of these combined. Techniques included here are beyond those related specifically to the script and writing at the letter level.

1. Writing lists كتابة قوائم

Purpose

To provide learners with practice writing at the word level. It requires little to no preparation and takes about 15 minutes to execute.

Procedure

1. Come up with a different everyday topic each time you want to use this technique, such as things your students need to shop for today or this week, different dishes they would like to eat during this week, or things they need to take with them on a trip.
2. Ask your students to write down a list of six items they need to shop for today or this week (such as food or clothing items) in 3–5 minutes.

Writing techniques 85

3. Divide the board into five columns and have five students come to the board and write down their lists of words.
4. Have each student read their list and elicit corrections of misspellings from all students in the class.
5. Repeat the process until all students have gone to the board and shared their lists with the class.
6. Invite students to ask questions about words they do not recognize or do not know.

Variations

a. Ask students to rank order the items in order of importance.
b. Instead of having your students write their lists on the board, display their lists via a document projector; have each student read their list off the document projector and go over them as a whole class.

2. *Fast copying* النسخ السريع

Purpose

To provide learners with practice writing at the word and phrase levels and pay attention to accurate writing and spelling. It requires little to no preparation and takes about 10 minutes to execute.

Procedure

1. Write on the board (or display via a screen or a document projector) 5–7 words and phrases that your students already know, in particular those that may be confusing for learners at this level or which they find challenging and are likely not to spell correctly, such as شوارع "streets," متخصّص "specialized," طاولة "big table," بنت طويلة "tall girl," بيت جميل "beautiful house", غرفة واسعة "spacious room," and others.
2. Instruct your students to look at the words and phrases on the board carefully before you will erase them in 30 seconds and that they will need to copy them (in no particular order) after you erase them at the 30-second mark.
3. Divide the boards into 3–5 columns and have students come to the board and write the words as they copied them.
4. Go over the words on the board as a whole class and elicit confirmation or corrections from all students in class.

Variations

a. To make the activity a little more challenging, include diacritics of internal short vowels and the *shadda* "geminate consonant symbol" and request students to copy all such diacritics along with the words.

86 Writing techniques

b. Give your students another chance to look at the words or to make corrections before going over their responses as a whole class by rewriting them on the board (or displaying them on a screen or via a document projector) and erasing them after 20 seconds.

(See also Harmer 2004.)

3. *Planning an itinerary* التخطيط لرحلة

Purpose

To provide learners with practice writing at the word and phrase levels. It allows for possibly integrating writing with reading and speaking. It requires little to no preparation and takes about 15 minutes to execute.

Procedure

1. Instruct your students that they will be going on a trip to five cities or states over a week or a 6-month period.
2. Ask them to plan their trip by day (or more specific time) or month and destination chronologically.
3. Divide your students into groups of dyads and have them exchange their itineraries to ask questions or offer corrections.
4. Have each student present their itinerary or have their partner do so for them.
5. Elicit corrections from the whole class for errors with the order of the days/ months and/or geographical locations of the cities/states.

Variations

a. Another suitable topic is to have your students write the weather forecast (using the Internet) over the coming days of the week.
b. Pre-teach your students key words related to the task if they do not know them.
c. Divide your students into groups of dyads and have them compare their forecasts for accuracy.

4. *Sentence modeling* النسج على منوال الجمل

Purpose

To provide learners with practice writing at the sentence level and promote writing fluency. It requires little to no preparation and takes about 15 minutes to execute.

Procedure

1. Prepare 1–2 typical sentences occurring in a given lesson at a time and ask your students to make up three sentences following the same pattern/structure and by

following the frames provided underneath each sentence (in 5–7 minutes) such as in the following samples:

> أ.   في الحَقيقة، لا تَتَذَكَّرُ أَسْماءَ كُلّ الأَفْرادِ في العائِلَة.
> 1—في الحَقيقة، لا _____ أَسْماءَ كُلّ _____ في _____.
> 2—في الحَقيقة، لا _____ أَسْماءَ كُلّ _____ في _____.
> 3—في الحَقيقة، لا _____ أَسْماءَ كُلّ _____ في _____.
>
> ب. لا تُحِبُّ هيوستن بِسَبَبِ الجوِّ الحارِّ في الصَّيف.
> 1- لا _____ _____ بِسَبَبِ الجوِّ _____ في _____.
> 2- لا _____ _____ بِسَبَبِ الجوِّ _____ في _____.
> 3- لا _____ _____ بِسَبَبِ الجوِّ _____ في _____.

2. Go over sample responses (one from each student) as a whole class and elicit corrections from all students
3. Collect your students' sentences for feedback and corrections later.

Variations

a. Include more sentence to be modeled, limiting the frames to be filled to one for each sentence and including fewer words within a frame as in the following samples:

> 1- في الحَقيقة، لا تَتَذَكَّرُ أَسماءَ كُلّ الأَفْرادِ في العائِلَة .
> في الحَقيقة، لا _____ أَسْماءَ _____ في _____.
>
> 2- لا تُحِبُّ هيوستن بِسَبَبِ الجوِّ الحارِّ في الصَّيف.
> لا _____ _____ بِسَبَبِ _____ في _____.
>
> 3- لي عَمٌّ اسْمُهُ خالِد يَسْكُنُ في مَدينة واشِنطُن .
> لي عَمَّةٌ _____ _____ في _____.

b. Instruct your students that they may have to make any necessary (grammatical) changes if the resulting frames allow for the possibility of different pronouns and/or verb conjugations (i.e., not simply copying the words from the model sentence, as in Sentence 3).
c. Divide your students into dyads and have them discuss their sentences and incorporate their partners' comments if they agree before going over the sentences as a whole class.

88   Writing techniques

5.   *Writing a long sentence* إنشاء جملة طويلة

Purpose

To provide learners with practice writing at the sentence level and promote writing fluency. It allows for the integration of writing with, possibly, reading and listening. It requires no preparation and takes about 10–15 minutes to execute, depending on the number of students in the class.

Procedure

1. Have students seated in a semicircle.
2. Instruct your students they are to collectively write a sentence and make it as long as they possibly can with each student contributing one word (which can be a verb, a noun, a pronoun, a preposition, etc.) in a chain fashion.
3. The first student (to the right or to the left) can name any person or thing as the first part of the sentence and write it on a sheet of paper and then passes it on to the next student.
4. The next student adds a word and passes the sheet of paper to the next student and so on.
5. Once a sentence reaches the limit and your students cannot make it longer, start over with another sentence so that all students can contribute to constructing a long sentence.
6. Once all students contributed to the construction of one or more sentences, go over the long sentence(s) as a whole class (e.g., by displaying each sentence to the class on the board, screen or via a document projector) and eliciting corrections from all students.

Variations

a. Instead of writing the words (making up a long sentence) on a sheet of paper, have a student come to the board and write the words as they heard them until a long sentence is completed.
b. Delegate another student to write the words on the board to make up the next sentence and so on.
c. All other students help the student writing on the board with writing and spelling errors.

6.   *Creative dictation* الإملاء الإبداعي

Purpose

To provide learners with practice writing at the sentence level and promote writing fluency. It allows for the integration of writing with listening. It requires little preparation and takes about 10–15 minutes to execute.

Writing techniques   89

Procedure

1. Prepare 4–5 typical sentences from a given lesson or ones containing vocabulary and structure which your students have already covered.
2. Instruct your students that they are to hear a dictation of 4–5 sentences that they are required to write down correctly and are allowed to replace a few words with ones to refer to them personally or to fit new possible and meaningful adaptations of the original dictated sentences but without changing the structure/pattern of the sentences, such as replacing some or all of the underlined words in the following sample sentences:

> ١ـ في الحَقيقة، لا تَتَذَكَّرُ أَسماءَ كُلِّ الأَفْرادِ في العائِلة.
>
> في الحَقيقة، لا أَتذَكَّرُ أَسماءَ كُلِّ الأَفْرادِ في الصَّفِ.
>
> ٢ـ لا تُحِبُّ هيوستن بِسَبَبِ الجوِّ الحارِّ في الصَّيفِ.
>
> لا نُحِبُّ بوسطن بِسَبَبِ الجوِّ البارِدِ في الشِّتاء.
>
> ٣ـ لِي عَمٌّ اسْمُهُ خالِد يَسْكُنُ في مَدينة واشِنطُن.
>
> لِي عَمّةٌ اسْمُها كيلي تَسْكُنُ في مَدينة بوفالو.

3. Instruct your students that when they replace anything, they should check if they need to make any additional necessary changes so that the new version of the sentence is grammatically correct.
4. Allow enough time between sentences for your students to hear the sentences, replace some or all of the target words, and make any additional required changes.
5. Go over your students' sentences (sentence by sentence) by having each student write the sentence on the board and elicit confirmation and corrections from all students in the class.

Variations

a. To save time, display the sentences of each student via a document projector and have the student writer read their sentences (sentence by sentence) and elicit confirmation or corrections from all class.
b. If time does not permit going over all students' dictations, go over a few sample dictations and collect your students' written dictations for grading and/or corrections later.

(See also Brookes and Grundy 1998.)

7. *Sentence completion* إكمال الجمل

Purpose

To provide learners with practice writing at the sentence level and promote writing fluency of sentential structure. It allows for the integration of writing

90 Writing techniques

with reading. It requires little preparation and takes about 15 minutes to execute.

Procedure

1. Prepare 4–5 typical sentences occurring in a current lesson and use them as a basis for providing incomplete sentences for your students to complete as in the following sample sentences:

١- أَدْرُس _____ .

٢- والِدِي يَعْمَل _____ .

٣—والِدَتِي _____ .

٤—لِي خَالة _____ .

٥—أَنا فِعْلًا _____ .

---

2. Instruct your students to complete the words provided into complete sentences with any number of words, including the use of one word so long as the outcomes are full meaningful sentences (in 8–10 minutes).
3. Instruct your students not to change the order of the words provided (i.e., to keep the words in the beginning of the sentences).
4. Go over the sentences as a whole class, with students reading their sentences (one sentence at a time in a chain fashion), and provide corrections as needed.
5. This can also be implemented as a dictation activity in which you dictate the beginning part and your students complete them into sentences.

Variations

a. Divide your students into groups of dyads and have them read and discuss their sentences with their partners.
b. Include a word count or range of words needed to complete the sentences, either one for each sentence or one for all the sentences across the board.

8. *Rearranging scrambled words within sentences*

إعادة ترتيب الكلمات المبعثرة في جمل

Purpose

To provide learners with practice writing at the sentence level and promote writing fluency of sentential structure. It requires little preparation and takes about 15 minutes to execute.

Procedure

1. Upon completing a lesson or unit in your students' textbook, prepare 4–5 typical sentences occurring in the lesson after modifying them slightly and scrambling

the order of words within the sentences such as in the following sample
sentences:

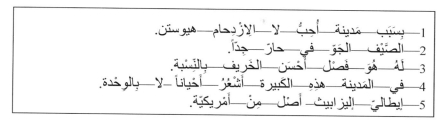

2. Distribute copies of a handout containing the sentences and ask your students to individually rearrange the words into sentences appropriately (in 8 minutes).
3. Divide your students into groups of dyads and have them discuss their reordered sentences and make any changes if they agree with their partners, although they do not always have to agree (in 4 minutes).
4. Go over the sentences as a whole class, with each group reading a sentence and students from other groups providing corrections.

Variations

a. Instead of groups reading their sentences, divide the board into five columns (and number them accordingly) and have each group delegate a student to go to the board and write one of the sentences.
b. Prepare a teacher's copy of the sentences where the correct sentences are provided underneath their respective scrambled sentences to display via a document project to confirm students' responses.

9. Similar and dissimilar متشابهان ومختلفان

Purpose

To provide learners with practice writing and improve their writing fluency, as they are required to write instantly about what they are presented. It allows for writing to be integrated with, possibly, the speaking skill. It requires little preparation and takes about 25 minutes to execute.

Procedure

1. Prepare a series of pictures of two separate daily routines of a female and a male sharing similar activities in some and differing in others, such as the samples displayed as in Figures 2–3:

92 Writing techniques

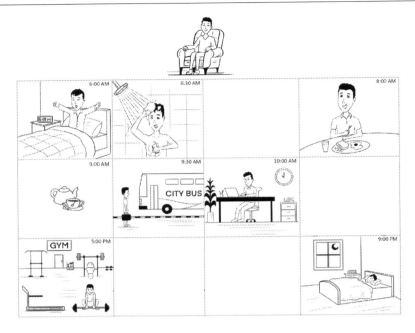

Figure 2 © Mohammed Alshehri

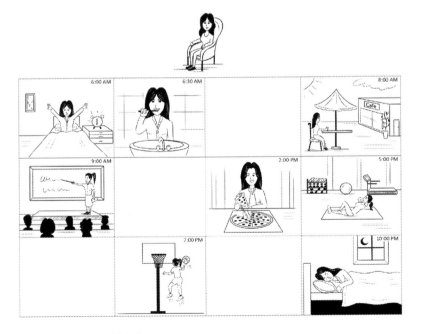

Figure 3 © Mohammed Alshehri

2. Divide students into dyads and have one partner write down 3–4 activities (in complete sentences) that the two characters share in common and the other partner write down 3–4 activities in which they differ, adding all details available (in 6–8 minutes).
3. Ask partners within their groups to discuss their sentences and agree on their written responses (in 5–7 minutes).
4. As a whole class, go over the sample responses (as many as time permits) and invite further refinement or corrections from all students in class.
5. Collect your students' drafts for feedback and corrections later.

Variations

a. Pictures can also be presented as discrete ones, and students are then asked to put them chronologically in the right order and write a sentence on each one.
b. Another topic can be past events (if students have learned the past tense) in which a male and a female character went on a trip during the last 1–2 weeks, such as the samples displayed in Figures 4–5:

Figure 4 (Adapted from Going Places, Burton and Maharg 1995, 141, 159)

94 Writing techniques

Figure 5 (Adapted from Going Places, Burton and Maharg 1995, 141, 159)

10. Likes and dislikes مرغوبات ومكروهات

Purpose

To provide learners with practice writing and improve their writing fluency, as they are required to write instantly and convey in writing basic functions of expressing likes and dislikes about topics of immediate interest. It allows for writing to be integrated with, possibly, speaking and reading. It requires no preparation and takes about 25 minutes to execute.

Procedure

1. Ask your students to select a topic of immediate interest to them such as food, traveling, sports, and so on.
2. Divide students into dyads and have one partner write four sentences (two long and two short) of what they like about the topic and the other write four sentences

Writing techniques 95

(two long and two short) of what they dislike about it; limit the short sentence to 3–5 words and the long sentence to more than 5 words (in 8 minutes).

3. Ask partners within their groups to discuss their sentences, allowing them to offer their feedback and comments (in 6–8 minutes).
4. Allow everyone to incorporate their partners' feedback and comments.
5. Have each student read out the long sentence and the short sentence written by their partner that they liked the most.
6. Collect your students' writings for feedback and corrections later.

Variations

a. Have each student write four short sentences (3–5 words) of likes and four short sentences of dislikes.
b. Divide your students into dyads and have partners discuss their sentences and make 4 of their 8 sentences they wrote to be long (more than 5 words).

(Brookes and Grundy 1998)

2. Developing writing at the intermediate level

At the intermediate level, writing involves production at the sentence and paragraph levels. At the intermediate level, learners of Arabic will benefit greatly from continued writing practice in isolation. However, it may also be useful at sometimes to implement techniques that integrate writing with one or more skills as is done in some of the techniques included here. Nonetheless, writing is viewed as a process rather than a product. To simplify things, a writing technique can be implemented as a pre-drafting, during drafting, post-drafting activity, or all of these combined. To provide feedback and corrections to students at the intermediate level, it is best if students are enabled to identify the corrections needed by using correction symbols and providing them with a simplified list of correction symbols such as the one in Appendix A.

11. *Rearranging and modifying scrambled sentences* إعادة ترتيب الجمل المبعثرة مع تغيير ما يلزم

Purpose

To provide learners with practice to develop their writing at the sentence and paragraph levels and promote their writing fluency of connecting basic ideas and statements in a text. It allows for the integration of writing with reading. It requires little preparation and takes about 20–25 minutes to execute.

Procedure

1. Find a level-appropriate text of a short paragraph of interest or relevance to your students or select one from your students' textbook which they have recently covered such as the following text:

> الأُسْتاذة سَميرة النَّجَّار مِصْرِيَّة. الْتَحَقَتْ بِجامِعة القاهِرة، ودَرَسَتْ فيها اللُّغة الفَرَنْسِيَّة. ثُمَّ أصْبَحَتْ مُتَرْجِمة. تَزَوَّجَتْ بَعْدَ حُصولِها عَلى وَظيفة مُتَرْجِم في وِزارة السِّياحة. بعد زَواجِها أنْجَبَتْ وَلَدَيْن. ابْنُها الكَبير أحْمَد يُحَضِّرُ لِشهادة الماجِسْتير في الجامِعة، وابْنُها الصَّغير سالِم طالِب في الصَّفّ الثَّاني الإعْدادي. أحْمَد يُحِبُّ قِراءة قِصَص المُغامَرات. وسالِم يَسْتَمْتِعُ بِالقِراءة أيْضاً، لكِنَّهُ يُحِبُّ الرِّياضة أكْثَر.

2. Type the sentences occurring in the text, placing them scrambled randomly one sentence on a separate line, adding redundant elements such as repeating the subjects of (verbal) sentences, and replacing pronouns with nouns as illustrated in the scrambled sentences of the following text:

> 1. دَرَسَتْ سَميرة في جامِعة القاهِرة اللُّغة الفَرَنْسِيّة.
>
> 2. الْتَحَقَتْ سَميرة بِجامِعة القاهِرة.
>
> 3. لكِن سالِم يُحِبُّ الرِّياضة أكْثَر.
>
> 4. بعد زَواجِها أنْجَبَتْ وَلَدَيْن.
>
> 5. أحْمَد يُحِبُّ قِراءة قِصَص المُغامَرات.
>
> 6. الأُسْتاذة سَميرة النَّجَّار مِصْرِيّة.
>
> 7. تَزَوَّجَتْ سَميرة بعد حُصولِها على وَظيفة مُتَرْجِم في وِزارة السِّياحة.
>
> 8. أصْبَحَتْ سَميرة مُتَرْجِمة.
>
> 9. اِبْن سَميرة الصَّغير سالِم طالِب في الصَّفّ الثَّاني الإعْدادي.
>
> 10. سالِم يَسْتَمْتِعُ بِالقِراءة أيْضاً.
>
> 11. اِبْن سَميرة الكَبير أحْمَد يُحَضِّرُ لِشهادة الماجِسْتير في الجامِعة.

3. Ask your students to individually read the sentences and arrange them into a coherent paragraph, making any necessary changes, such as deleting all redundant subject nouns and replacing others with pronouns, and adding any appropriate connectors such as ثُمَّ "then" and و "and" when necessary (12–15 minutes).

4. Divide your students into dyads and have them discuss their responses (6–8 minutes).

5. Go over your students' responses as a whole class by having, for example, each sentence read by a different student or group and inviting other students to confirm or disconfirm if the sentence is in the right order as well as the proper choice of verb conjugation.

6. Allow a different order of sentences or a different connector if the order or connector is appropriate.

Variations

a. Divide your students into dyads from the beginning to collaborate on putting the sentences in the right order, making all necessary changes, and adding an appropriate connector when necessary.
b. Pre-teach basic punctuation rules involving the use of the period and comma if your students do not already know them.
c. Another suitable topic is to have the sentences of a cooking recipe scrambled, but since this has to do with a process and specific vocabulary, it can be best given to students at a higher level.

12. *Brainstorming and fast drafting* استثارة الأفكار والإنشاء السريع

Purpose

To provide learners with practice to develop their writing at the sentence and paragraph levels and promote their writing fluency of connecting basic ideas and statements in a text. It allows for the integration of writing with reading and speaking. It requires no preparation and takes about 25–30 minutes to execute.

Procedure

1. Come up with a topic of interest or relevance to your students, such as food, sports, friendship, living in a big city, traveling, and so on; you can make any of these topics more tangible and specific by asking your students to each, for example, come up with a reason why people like or need food, why people like sports, why people prefer to live in a big city rather than a small city, why traveling is enjoyable, and so on.
2. Ask your students to individually write one idea on the topic on a sheet of paper (5 minutes).
3. Collect the sheets in a bag or box and shuffle them.
4. Divide your students into groups of 5.
5. Ask each group to pick up five sheets (each containing one idea) and work as a group to combine the ideas into a short coherent paragraph, making all needed changes and adding appropriate connectors such as ثُمَّ "then" and و "and" (10–15 minutes).
6. Go over each group's draft as a whole class by displaying each draft via a document projector and having one student delegated by the group read the paragraph to the class.
7. Elicit corrections from all students in class when needed.
8. Collect the groups' drafts for additional comments and corrections later.

98   Writing techniques

Variations

a. Have each student write their idea on the board and number the ideas so it is easy to divide them among the students.
b. Don't allow any previously written idea on the board to be repeated.
c. Divide the ideas among the groups of 5, with 5 ideas each.
d. Have groups exchange their drafts with at least another group to receive feedback and comments.
e. Allow time (5 minutes) for each group to incorporate the feedback and comments they received from other groups.

(See also Harmer 2004.)

13.   *Transforming a dialogue into a narrative paragraph*
تحويل حوار إلى نصّ سرديّ

Purpose

To provide learners with practice to develop their writing at the sentence and paragraph levels and promote their writing fluency of moving between dialogue and direct speech into narrative, indirect/reported speech. It allows for the integration of writing with reading and speaking. It requires little to no preparation and takes about 30–35 minutes to execute.

Procedure

1. Find an appropriate-level dialogue (about 1 page) of interest or relevance to your students or select one from your students' textbook.
2. Go over key vocabulary such as قالَ إنَّ ... "he said that," سألَه/ـها هل ... "he asked him/her if," أضافَ أنّ، "he added that," and so on.
3. Divide your students into dyads.
4. Instruct your students within groups to transform the dialogue into a narrative paragraph by converting each turn of the dialogue into reported speech (15–20 minutes).
5. Go over sample drafts of your students' narrative paragraphs as a whole class by delegating a student from each group to read the paragraph (while displaying it to the class via a document projector) and eliciting corrections from all students in class.

Variations

a. Instruct your students to summarize the dialogue in their own words in 40–50 words as a way to get the gist of the dialogue to report it to a third party.
b. Have groups exchange their drafted paragraphs to provide comments and corrections at least once with another group.

Writing techniques 99

c. Allow your students time to incorporate the comments and corrections received from another group before going over the drafts as a whole class.
d. Instead of converting a dialogue into a narrative paragraph, have your students convert a suitable narrative text into a dialogue.

14. *My daily routine* نشاطاتي اليومية

Purpose

To provide learners with practice writing at the sentence and paragraph levels and improve their writing fluency, as they are required to write within a limited time. It allows for writing to be integrated with the speaking skill. It requires no preparation and takes about 30–35 minutes to execute.

Procedure

1. Ask each student to write down the activities of their daily routine (consisting of 8–10 habitual activities) from the morning when they wake up to the evening when they go to sleep in no more than 8–10 minutes.
2. Divide students into dyads to discuss their daily routine with each other and write down the activities of their partner that they do not do in 8–10 minutes (this will allow them to express negation in the present tense).
3. Have each student finalize a written narrative of their daily routine in a short paragraph (about 150 words), including those that they do and those that they do not do, unlike their partners, and adding adverbial expressions (أو لا/في البداية "at first," في الصباح "in the morning," عند الظهر "at noon," بعد الظهر "after noon," في المساء "in the evening," أخيراً "at last," etc.) as well as connectors to introduce their sentences (و "and," ثمَّ "then," بعد ذلك "after that," etc.) in 8–10 minutes.
4. Go over in class 1–2 good sample responses and invite further refinement or correction from class.
5. Collect your students' drafts for feedback and corrections later.

Variations

a. Another topic can be how they spent the previous weekend (Saturday or Sunday) or a recent trip they had out of town.
b. Accordingly, the ultimate written paragraph will be about past events that they did and did not do; that is, in comparison with those of their partners within dyads (this will allow them to express negation in the past tense).
c. If time permits, or in a subsequent class, have each student present what they wrote orally, allowing them to glance at what they wrote occasionally.

100 Writing techniques

15. *Personal letters, notes, and postcards* كتابة رسائل خاصة وملحوظات وبطاقات بريدية

Purpose

To provide learners with practice writing and improve their writing fluency, as they are encouraged to communicate quickly and informally via email and other means about personal matters, mimicking real-life situations. These situations include writing personal letters/emails, postcards, and notes. It requires no preparation and allows possibly for the integration of writing with reading and speaking. It takes about 20–25 minutes to execute.

Procedure

1. Each time you implement this technique, come up with a different practical reason for writing personal letters/emails/texts (e.g., to invite a friend to dinner, watch a movie together, or to inform them about an important decision they have made), notes (e.g., as thank-you notes for a gift they have sent them, for visiting them while they were sick, or for their well-wishes; as actual notes for their roommate that they have left the house to go shopping, to give a friend a ride somewhere, or to pick up someone from the airport), and postcards (e.g., to mail to friends or family members while traveling to a resort, historical site, or abroad).
2. Your students should bring their laptops or smartphones to class (or they can use paper and pencil).
3. Come up with a defined topic such as writing an email to a friend to invite them to dinner.
4. Go over some key vocabulary for the task if necessary.
5. Divide your students into dyads so they can write the letters to each other, pretending they are friends in real life.
6. Ask your students to write the personal letter/email/text taking all the components of the letter into account, such as salutation, invitation statement (along with the time and place), concluding statement or question, and concluding salutation (in 8–10 minutes)
7. Each student reads their partner's letter/email/text and responds by accepting or declining the invitation (in 5 minutes).
8. Go over as a whole class samples of your students' letters and responses and elicit from students of other groups suggestions and corrections.
9. Have your students send you their email drafts for feedback and corrections later.

Variations

a. If computers and smartphones are not available, students can draft their correspondence via paper and pencil.
b. Limit the letter to a certain number of words (e.g., 25–30 words).

Writing techniques 101

16. *Sum it up* اكتبوا الخلاصة

Purpose

To provide learners with practice writing and improve their writing fluency at the sentence and paragraph levels. It allows for the integration of writing with speaking. It requires no preparation and takes about 30–35 minutes to execute.

Procedure

1. Upon reading a text (from your students' textbook or from outside the book) and answering comprehension questions on it, divide your students into two groups and have them sit in a semicircle.
2. Instruct each group to come up with a summary of the text by having each student within a group contribute an idea or sentence (in 10–15 minutes) by writing it down on a separate sheet and passing it on to another partner to do the same and so on.
3. Once all students within a group have contributed to the summary and have exhausted all the ideas in the text, have them refine their sentences into a summary and make any final changes and modifications, including adding necessary connectors (in 5 minutes).
4. Have each group present their draft of the summary by delegating a student to read it (while displaying it via a document projector).
5. Allow students from other groups to provide comments or corrections.
6. Invite your students to ask any questions they have about the text or questions raised by the text or newly drafted summaries.

Variations

a. Allow the groups to exchange their drafts to provide and receive comments and corrections from at least one other group.
b. Allow groups to incorporate comments and corrections received from other groups before going over the drafted summaries as a whole class.
c. Have an all-class vote on the best summary.

17. *Reconstructing a story* إعادة إنشاء قصة

Purpose

To provide learners with practice to develop their writing and promote their writing fluency at the sentence and paragraph levels and connect their sentences within a paragraph. It allows for the integration of writing with reading, listening, and speaking. It requires little preparation and takes about 35–40 minutes to execute.

102   Writing techniques

Procedure

1. Prepare a story outline of a known short story for your students, consisting of five correctly (chronologically) ordered sections.
2. Distribute a copy of the outline to each student.
3. Divide your students into dyads and assign each a specific part of the outline.
4. Instruct groups to reconstruct their parts of the story with a word limit of 40–50 words each (in 15 minutes).
5. Have sets of five dyads discuss their parts and work on connecting their reconstructed parts together, adding necessary connectors (in 10–15 minutes).
6. Have each set of five groups present their draft of the reconstructed story by delegating a student to read it (while displaying it via a document projector).
7. Allow other students from other groups to provide comments or corrections.

Variations

a. To make the activity a little more challenging, scramble the order of the sections within the outline and have each set of groups of 5 work on connecting their parts as well as putting them in the right order.
b. Reward the groups that provided a more accurate reconstruction of the story and fewest writing and grammatical errors.

(See also Brookes and Grundy 1998.)

18. *Completing a story* إكمَال قِصَّة

Purpose

To provide learners with practice to develop their writing and promote their writing fluency at the sentence and paragraph levels. It allows for the integration of writing with, possibly, reading, listening, and speaking. It requires little preparation and takes about 30–35 minutes to execute.

Procedure

1. Prepare a short paragraph or a long sentence introducing the first part of a short story, omitting the second part/ending; the beginning should end with a proper cliff-hanger such as in the following sample:

> زَعَموا أَنَّ أَسَداً كانَ في غابَةٍ مُجاوِرَةٍ لِطَريقٍ مِنْ طُرُق النّاس، وكانَ لَهُ أَصْحابٌ ثَلاثَةٌ: ذِئْبٌ وغُرابٌ وابْنُ آوَى، وأَنَّ رُعاةً مَرُّوا بِذلِكَ الطَّريق. فَتَخَلَّفَ جَمَلٌ، ولَمْ يَعرِفْ مِنْ أَينَ يَذْهَبُ، ودَخَلَ غابَة الأَسَد . . .

2. Instruct your students to individually write a paragraph (around 75 words) concluding the story of what, for example, will happen to the camel, in this case (in

Writing techniques   103

15 minutes); the concluding part should be logical and follow naturally from the beginning part as much as possible.

3. Divide your students into dyads and have each student read their draft to their partner (in 10 minutes).
4. Allow partners to ask questions or provide comments or corrections.
5. Go over in class sample drafts (by having each student read their paragraph while displaying it via a document projector) and elicit comments and corrections from all students in class.
6. Collect your students' drafts for feedback and corrections later.

Variations

a. Instead of having students complete the last part of the story, omit the first part of the story and present them with the second/last part and ask them to write a beginning part of the story.
b. Have students work on drafting the paragraphs in dyads.
c. Reward the writer(s) of the draft with the most logical conclusion (or beginning part) and fewest writing and grammatical errors.

19. *Paraphrasing a text to simplify it* إعادة صَوغ نصّ لتسهيله

Purpose

To provide learners with practice writing and improve their writing fluency. It allows for writing to be integrated, possibly, with speaking and reading. It requires little to no preparation and takes about 30–35 minutes to execute.

Procedure

1. Select a text in your students' textbook or a text which you have recently covered in class and your students have understood its content and intent; if the text consists of more than one paragraph, select one paragraph.
2. Divide your students into 1–3 groups, each group consisting of a number of students equivalent to the number of sentences in the paragraph.
3. Ask groups to paraphrase the text with each student responsible for paraphrasing one sentence in their own words so that students at a level below theirs can understand it (in 10 minutes).
4. Have each group discuss their paraphrased sentences collectively and mold them into one paragraph, making all changes that they agree on (in 10 minutes).
5. Have each group report their paraphrased version to class, inviting any follow-up questions or comments from other groups (in 10–15 minutes).
6. Reward the group whose version is the closest to the original text.
7. Collect your students' responses for further feedback and corrections.

104   Writing techniques

Variations

a. Prepare your own version paraphrasing the text and use it as a baseline against which to evaluate your students' responses.
b. Display your version to class on a screen or via the document projector.
c. Exchange students' versions among groups (for feedback and comments) before going over them as a whole class; allow groups time to incorporate other groups' comments and corrections.
d. Have your students vote on which version is closest to yours.

(See also Brookes and Grundy 1998.)

20. *Discussing job announcements/advertisements* مناقشة إعلانات وظائف

Purpose

To provide learners with practice writing and improve their writing fluency, as they are encouraged to communicate quickly and informally via email. It requires little preparation and allows possibly for the integration of writing with reading and speaking. It takes about 40 minutes to execute.

Procedure

1. Prepare two job announcements/advertisements, such as working as a translator, working at the library, working at an office as a secretary, working at a restaurant, and the like.
2. Your students should bring their laptops or smartphones to class (or prearrange for your students to attend class in a computer lab).
3. Distribute copies of the two job advertisements.
4. Go over some key vocabulary in the two job advertisements that your students may not know.
5. Divide your students into dyads and have each write two short paragraphs—one about the similarities and one about the differences of the two job advertisements (in terms of working hours, suitability, location, pay, benefits, etc.)—and email it to their partner (in 15 minutes).
6. Each student reads their partner's paragraphs and responds via email if their partner missed any of the similarities or differences and adds other comments or any issues with the job advertisements (in 10 minutes).
7. Each student incorporates their partners' comments which they agree on (in 5 minutes).
8. Go over in class 1–2 good sample responses and invite comments from students of other groups.
9. Have your students send you their email drafts for feedback and corrections later.

Writing techniques   105

Variations

a. If computers and smartphones are not available, your students can use paper and pencil and exchange them with their partners.
b. The writing can be limited to one paragraph in the form of advice where a student starts their draft by informing their partner (in writing) which job is more suitable (for them or for their partner) and then explains why. The "why" part should focus on the similarities and differences between the two job advertisements.

3. Developing writing at the advanced level

At the advanced level, writing involves production at the paragraph and extended discourse levels and ranges from the use of high-frequency vocabulary and structures to the use of low-frequency (and specialized) vocabulary and (more complex) structures. At this stage, for pedagogical reasons and to maximize classroom time for language development, techniques used are expected to integrate writing with one or more skills in addition to those which focus on writing in isolation. While using a form or function through a skill, learners can activate it or recycle it through another and achieve control and automaticity through others. Writing here is viewed as a process rather than a product. To simplify things, a writing technique can be implemented as a pre-drafting, during-drafting, post-drafting activity, or all of these combined. To provide feedback and corrections to students at the advanced level, it is best if students are enabled to identify the corrections needed by using correction symbols and providing them with a list of correction symbols such as the one in Appendix B.

21. *Applying for a job in response to a job advertisement*
التقدّم إلى عمل بناءً على إعلان لوظيفة

Purpose

To provide learners with practice writing and improve their writing fluency, as they are encouraged to communicate quickly and as accurately as possible to get the job. It requires little preparation and allows possibly for the integration of writing with reading and speaking. It takes about 30–40 minutes to execute.

Procedure

1. Prepare a job announcement/advertisement that requires academic and professional qualifications and experience; an Arabic job advertisement may include several different positions.
2. Go over the main components of a formal job letter in Arabic (including the addresses of the sender and addressee, a salutation, an introductory statement stating the sender is applying for a particular job, a paragraph stating the reason

106 Writing techniques

for application along with the qualifications and experience, a closing statement of thanking the addressee for considering the application, and a concluding salutation followed by the signature and name).

3. Go over any additional key vocabulary in the job advertisement.
4. Distribute copies of the job advertisement to your students.
5. Have each student write a job letter in response to the advertisement and, if the advertisement includes several positions, state for which position the application letter is in about 100 words (in 15 minutes).
6. Go over in class a few sample drafts and invite corrections with respect to any missing components, missing information, and writing and style errors.
7. Reward the writer of the most complete draft with the fewest style and writing errors.

Variations

a. Divide your students into dyads and have them present the letter to their partners, inviting feedback and corrections.
b. Allow your students to incorporate their partners' comments and corrections.

22. *Writing under time pressure* الكتابة تحت تأثير ضغط الوقت

Purpose

To provide learners with practice writing and improve their writing fluency, as they are requested to write within a time limit. It boosts self-confidence, as it provides concrete guidelines for how to draft a paragraph while managing their time to complete the activity. It requires no preparation and takes about 30–40 minutes to execute.

Procedure

1. Ask your students to select a topic of interest such as sports, friendship, success, the environment, traveling, and so on.
2. Ask your students to define their selected topic in a well-organized paragraph, using proper connectors between sentences (i.e., beyond using the basic conjunction و "and") in 20 minutes.
3. Instruct your students to start by brainstorming for ideas and how to organize them (in 3–5 minutes) and allow an equal amount of time to double-check and edit their writing at the end.
4. Ask your students to provide specific examples to support their definitions within 5–7 sentences during the remaining time (10 minutes).
5. Divide students into dyads and have partners exchange their writings to read and provide feedback and comments (10 minutes).

Writing techniques   107

6. Allow everyone to incorporate their partners' feedback and comments.
7. Collect your students' drafts for feedback and corrections later.

Variations

a. Start the whole activity by dividing your students into dyads and have them brainstorm a topic of interest and agree on one to write about.
b. Have groups exchange their written paragraphs so that each group can receive at least one set of feedback and comments from one group.
c. If time permits, repeat the preceding step so that each group can receive more than one set of feedback and comments from other groups.
d. Allow each group enough time to read and incorporate other groups' feedback and comments.

(See also Oshima and Hogue 2006.)

23. *Differences and similarities* أوجه الشبه والاختلاف

Purpose

To provide learners with practice writing and improve their writing fluency beyond a paragraph, as they are requested to compare and contrast between two figures or entities. It requires little preparation and allows possibly for the integration of writing with reading and speaking. It takes about 40–45 minutes to execute.

Procedure

1. Come up with two biographies (2–3 paragraphs long or 1 page long each) of two historical or contemporary figures (statespersons, leaders, politicians, inventors, philosophers, thinkers, activists, writers, etc.).
2. Distribute copies of the biographies to each student.
3. Go over key vocabulary in the two biographical texts.
4. Divide your students into dyads and have them go over the two biographies and have one student write a list of (5–7) similarities and their partner write a list of (5–7) differences between the two figures (in 15–20 minutes).
5. Ask each student to expand their list into a coherent paragraph, using proper connectors to introduce their sentences and connect them with previous ones (in about 10 minutes).
6. Have each group discuss their two paragraphs for accuracy in content and form and incorporate them into one draft with the appropriate connector between the two paragraphs (in about 10 minutes).
7. Go over as a whole class a few sample drafts and elicit corrections for errors from students of other groups.
8. Collect your students' drafts for feedback and corrections later.

108   Writing techniques

Variations

a. Instead of comparing and contrasting between two figures, two entities (such as organizations, companies, universities, cities, etc.), two things (dishes, movies, books, sports, systems, policies, philosophies, etc.), or events (such as wars, disasters, revolutions, etc.) can be used.
b. If time permits, exchange drafts between groups and invite comments and corrections by other groups.

(See also Blanchard and Root 2010.)

24. *Reconstructing the article from article outline* إعادة صَوغ المقال من مخطط المقال

Purpose

To provide learners with practice writing and improve their writing fluency at the extended discourse level. It requires little to no preparation and allows possibly for the integration of writing with reading and speaking. It takes about 50–60 minutes to execute.

Procedure

1. Find an article (3–6 paragraphs) of interest or relevance to your students or select a text from their own textbooks which contains three obvious parts an introduction, a body, and a conclusion.
2. Divide your students into groups of 3 to go over the article and make a summary outline consisting of an introduction, a body, and a conclusion (in 15–20 minutes).
3. Ask each group to reconstruct the article based on their outline; each student within a group can be responsible for reconstructing a sub-component part so that one can work on the introduction, another on the body, and the third on the conclusion (in about 10 minutes).
4. Although students within each group can divide up the task of reconstructing the draft from the three component parts of the outline among themselves, the group is responsible collectively for the accuracy of the entire reconstructed draft; therefore, allow time for the group to edit their draft collectively (10 minutes).
5. Exchange drafts between groups and invite comments and corrections by other groups at least once (10–15 minutes).
6. Allow groups to consider the comments and corrections they received from another group as a second round for editing their draft (10 minutes).
7. Collect your students' drafts for feedback and corrections later.

Writing techniques **109**

Variations

a. Due to time constraints, it is best if this technique is implemented as a post-reading activity (whether it is based on a text from your students' textbook or outside of it) and you have already gone over it along with its comprehension questions and related activities.
b. After edits are made following your own feedback, have groups present their work in a subsequent class and compare their drafts with the original one.
c. Reward the group which reconstructed the closest draft to the original.

(See also Oshima and Hogue 2006.)

25. *Whole-class collaborative writing* الكتابة التعاونية على مستوى الصفّ

Purpose

To provide learners with practice writing and improve their writing fluency at the extended discourse level, including expressing (in writing) the functions of comparing and contrasting and supporting an opinion. It is best implemented as a pre-drafting and during-drafting activity. It requires little to no preparation and allows possibly for the integration of all skills: writing, reading, speaking, and listening. It takes about 50–60 minutes to execute.

Procedure

1. Come up with a topic of interest or relevance to your students such as using email for personal letters
2. As a warm-up, pre-drafting activity, ask class 3–5 general but guided questions, such as whether they use regular mail or email for their personal letters, when was the last time they wrote a letter through email, how long it took them to write that letter, whether they received a response yet, and whether they have a copy of the letter they sent, among others (in 5 minutes).
3. Divide the board into two columns/halves and label the right one محاسن استخدام البريد الإلكتروني للرسائل الشخصية "the advantages of using email for personal letters."
4. Elicit from the whole class three advantages of using email for personal letters and write them on the board (in 5 minutes).
5. Label the left column/half of the board مساوئ استخدام البريد الإلكتروني للرسائل الشخصية "the disadvantages of using email for personal letters."
6. Elicit from the whole class three disadvantages of using email for personal letters and write them on the board (in 5 minutes).
7. Divide your students into groups of 3–5 students.
8. Have each group brainstorm for three additional advantages and three additional disadvantages (in 10 minutes).

110 Writing techniques

9. Each group delegates a student to read their list of three advantages and list of three disadvantages aloud and another one to write them and add them to the lists on the board; the one writing on the board is not permitted to copy the group's lists from written notes but from listening to their partner who is reading the group's lists.
10. Groups are not allowed to repeat items already on the board.
11. The whole class is allowed to correct the student writing on the board.
12. Instruct groups that they are to write an outline of a composition topic of whether they prefer to use email for personal letters and why, brainstorming immediately, and using any of the items on the board (in 10 minutes).
13. Instruct your students to write their first draft consisting of two paragraphs (one on the advantages and the other on the disadvantages) based on the outline they made and ideas that they have just brainstormed (15–20 minutes).
14. Collect your students' drafts for feedback and corrections later.

Variations

a. If time permits, allow groups to exchange their drafts with other groups at least once, inviting comments and corrections.
b. Allow groups to incorporate other groups' comments and corrections into their drafts before submitting them.

Chapter 5

Grammar techniques

1. Developing grammatical competence at the novice level

While techniques for developing the four language skills and entailed functional abilities are essential for developing communicative competence within the communicative language teaching approach, techniques aimed to provide deliberate and purposeful practice for developing grammatical competence are equally important. Grammar techniques included in the novice level focus on grammatical forms (along with the meanings and functions that they entail) at the word (i.e., morphological), phrase, and sentence (syntactic and morphosyntactic) levels, which aim at developing grammar knowledge of the most basic and high-frequency forms. It is important whenever possible to integrate grammar techniques with those intended for developing language skills. Doing so has many added benefits including driving boredom out of the teaching of grammar, demonstrating to learners the important role of grammar in carrying meanings, and optimizing classroom time by also developing other skills.

1. Chain question formation صَوغ السؤال تسلسليًّا

Purpose

To provide deliberate practice in question formation, in particular questions involving ما "what," من "who," كيف "how," أين "where," and من أين "where from." It allows for the integration of deliberate grammar practice with the speaking skill. It requires little to no preparation and takes about 15 minutes to execute.

Procedure

1. Arrange classroom seats in a semicircle (or two semicircles one behind the other, depending on the number of students in the class).
2. Stand or sit where the right end of the semicircle is to your right and the left end to your left.

DOI: 10.4324/9781315686677-6

112 Grammar techniques

3. Turn to the student to your right or left; if turning to the student to your right, model the question with ما "what" by pointing to any object of the class; for example, point to a book in from of you, ask ما هذا؟ "What is this?" and elicit the response هذا كِتاب "This is a book."

4. Provide error correction by means of recast if a student, for example, produces the feminine form of the demonstrative rather than the masculine form or vice versa.

5. That student turns to the student to their right and asks them the same form of the question by pointing to a different object in the class.

6. The chain of questions continues in the same fashion until each student in the class has responded to the question of the previous student and asked the next student a question.

7. Reinforce the rule of question formation by writing 2–3 questions (or having some students write the questions they had produced) on the board and inviting any questions your students may have.

8. In the same way, question formation involving other question words/particles can be presented and practiced by modeling the following example of questions: أنا محمد، مَنْ أنتَ/أَنْتِ؟ "I am Muhammad; who are you?" كيف الحال/الدراسة/المدرسة أين الكتاب/الدفتر/القلم . . .؟ . . . "How are you/how is studying/school . . .?" . . . من أين أنتَ/أنتِ؟ "Where is the book/notebook/pen . . .?" "Where are you from?"

9. Use of the question أين "where" presupposes knowledge of some prepositions and adverbs of time; therefore, pre-teach such vocabulary when presenting and practicing question formation involving this particle.

Variations

a. This technique can be used to teach or review question words/particles one at a time.

b. Other question types using question words/particles such as أي "which," كم "how many," and لِمَ/لماذا "why" can be used toward the upper end of this level when each can be preceded by a yes/no question; thus, for example, the chain of question formation activity here (consisting of two sub-questions) starts with (هل) تحبّ/تحبّين الأفلام؟ "Do you like movies?" (using هل as the yes/no question particle or rising intonation) and upon answering in the affirmative, the follow-up question can be أيّ الأفلام تحبّ/تحبّين؟ "Which movies do you like?" or "How many movies do you watch per week?"; if the answer is in the negative, the follow-up question can be لِمَ/لماذا (لا تحبّ/تحبّين الأفلام)؟ "Why (don't you like movies)?"

c. Use pictures or slides containing pictures (with objects located in different places) that you display one by one and have students point to the objects in the pictures when asking each other.

Grammar techniques 113

d. Use a picture with objects located in different places together with a list of the objects below the picture and make copies for all students so students can make questions on all the items by turn.
e. Instead of pointing (whether to a real object or a picture of an object), hold an object (such as a book, notebook, a piece of paper, card, etc.) and place it somewhere and ask the next student where it is; after the student responds, hand them the object to place it anywhere they want in preparation of asking the next student where it is and so on.

2. *Describing pictures using noun-adjective phrases* وصف الصور باستخدام الصفة والموصوف

Purpose

To provide deliberate practice in phrasal (noun–adjective) structure formation and involved agreement in gender, number, definiteness, and case. It allows for the integration of deliberate grammar practice with, possibly, the writing and speaking skills. It is best implemented after learners have already been presented with the construction. It requires little to no preparation and takes about 15–20 minutes to execute.

Procedure

1. Prepare 1–3 pictures with objects or persons with distinct attributes to be displayed on the board, screen, or via a document projector
2. Divide your students into dyads and ask each group to write down as many complete sentences as possible, using noun-adjective phrases at least 2 sentences (in about 5 minutes).
3. Go over students' written sentences as a whole class by having each group first write their sentences on the board (or displaying them via a document projector) and then reading them.
4. Invite students from other groups to provide corrections.

Variations

a. Provide each group with a different picture so that your students can generate many different sentences.
b. Alternatively, prepare a set of two similar pictures wherein objects can be readily compared and contrasted.
c. Instead of pictures, request each student/group to find a specific item in the classroom and make up 1–2 complete sentences, using proper attributive adjectives of the item (within noun–adjective phrases).

114   Grammar techniques

3. *Find the relations between words* ابحثوا عن العلاقات بين الكلمات

Purpose

To provide deliberate practice in *'idāfa* structure formation and the possessed–possessor relationship between referents of words in this construction. It allows for the integration of deliberate grammar practice with, possibly, the speaking skill. It is best implemented after learners have already been presented with the *'idāfa* construction. It requires little to no preparation and takes about 5–10 minutes to execute.

Procedure

1. Prepare 2–3 *'idāfa* phrases consisting of 5–8 words each, such as the following:

    a. key, door, car, couch, team, football, and university to form
       مفتاح باب سيارة مدرّب فريق كرة قدم جامعة
    b. drawer, table, office, secretary, school, and languages to form
       دُرج طاولة مكتب سكرتيرة مدرسة لغات
    c. parking, cars, employees, company, and telephones to form
       موقف سيارات موظفي شركة تلفونات/هواتف

2. Include each word (in Arabic) on an index card on one side and a picture of it on the other side.

3. Divide your students into groups of 5–8 reflecting the number of words in the *'idāfa* phrases you had prepared on the index cards and have them assemble the words in the right order, reflecting a possessed–possessor relation from right to left (in 3 minutes).

4. Go over your students' responses as a whole class after each group delegates a student to write the phrase on the board.

5. Reinforce two of the rules of the *'idāfa* structure by asking your students why the sound masculine plural word did not occur as موظّفون "employees" but occurred here as موظّفي (i.e., with the genitive case ending and final consonant [n] deleted).

6. Ask each group to make their phrase definite according to the rules of *'idāfa* that they have learned (i.e., by making the last noun definite or adding a proper name at the end of the phrase such as "Michigan" to phrase [a] above) in no more than 30 seconds.

7. Go over your students' responses as a whole class, eliciting corrections from students in other groups.

Variations

a. Provide words in each phrase together scrambled randomly (on a handout or displayed on the board, screen, or via a document projector) so that phrase

(a) above would look like the following: مفتاح—باب—كرة قدم—سيارة—فريق جامعة—مدرّب -

b. Pre-teach any vocabulary item(s) that your students may not know.

c. To be sure your students understood the concept of *'idāfa* structure well, ask them to demonstrate the notion of possessed–possessor relations by asking each group to line up in front of the class in the correct order (e.g., from left to right with the one immediately possessed/owned by the other to stand to their left or vice versa), with each one stating (starting from the one standing to the far left) عندي "I have" so that for phrase (a), for example, the student who has the "university" card would say عندي فريق كرة قدم "I have a football team," the one who has the card of the "football team" would say عندي مدرّب "I have a couch," the student who has the "couch" card would say عندي سيّارة "I have a car," and so on.

4. *Chain question formation and the use of adverbials*
صَوغ السؤال تسلسليًا واستخدام الظروف

Purpose

To provide deliberate practice in question formation involving مَتى "when" and the use of adverbials of time and place in the responses. It allows for the integration of deliberate grammar practice with the speaking skill. It requires little preparation and takes about 15 minutes to execute.

Procedure

1. Pre-teach adverbs of time using تنوين النصب "*nunation* of the accusative case" such as صباحاً "in the morning," ظهراً "noon," مساءً "in the evening," يوميّاً "daily," أسبوعيّاً "weekly," شهريّاً "monthly," and so on and some equivalent phrases using the preposition في "in" for adverbs such as في الصباح "in the morning," في المساء "in the evening."

2. Arrange the seats in class in a semicircle (or two semicircles one behind the other, depending on the number of students in the class).

3. Stand or sit where the right end of the semicircle is to your right and the left end to your left.

4. Turn to the student to your right or left; if turning to the student to your right, model the question with مَتى "when" by stating أنا أشرب القهوة في الصباح "I drink coffee in the morning" and then asking متى تشرب/تشربين القهوة؟ "When do you drink coffee?"

5. That student turns to the student to their right and asks them a similar question using مَتى "when" about anything else.

116 Grammar techniques

6. The chain of questions continues in the same fashion until each student in the class has responded to the question of the previous student and asked the next student a similar question.
7. Reinforce the rule of question formation by writing 2–3 questions (or having some students write the questions they had produced) on the board and inviting any questions your students may have.

Variations

a. Prepare a series of pictures (to use on slides/screen or via a document projector) of individuals conducting daily activities at a certain time of the day or on certain occasions.
b. Pre-teach telling the time, at least the basic forms, if you indicate the time of the activity in the picture as an optionally additional time reference your students can use.

5. *Find related words by root and pattern* إبحثوا عن الكلمات المشتقة من الجذر والوزن نفسيهما

Purpose

To provide learners with deliberate practice in identifying words that share the same roots and patterns to help them guess word meanings (as a robust strategy with which the strategy of guessing word meanings from context can be combined) in order to promote their bottom-up processing of texts. It allows for the integration of deliberate grammar practice with the reading skill. It requires little preparation and takes about 15 minutes to execute.

Procedure

1. Find a level-appropriate text or a little higher (of one short paragraph) or select one from your students' textbook such as the following text:

> بَعْدَ نَجاحي في الصَّفّ الثاني عَشَر دَخَلْتُ كُلِّيَة الطِّب في جامِعة دِمَشْق. كانَتْ تِلْكَ رَغْبَتي دائماً. والِدي كانَ يُريدُني أن أَدْخُل كُلِّيَة التِّجارة لكِنَّه لم يَرْفُض دُخولي كُلِّيَة الطِّب. والِدَتي كانَتْ تَرْغَب في الْتِحاقي بكُلِّيَة الطِّب لأكون طَبيبة مِثْلها ومِثْل جَدّي. تَخَرَّجْتُ وحَصَلْتُ على تَقْدير جَيِّد بَعْدَ سَبْع سَنَوات طَويلة مِن الدِّراسة. بعد تَخَرُّجي، ساعَدَتْني صَديقة والِدَتي في الحُصول على عَمَل مَعَها في مَشْفى الرَّازي والإنْتِساب إلى جَمْعِيّة الأطِبّاء السّوريين.

2. Prepare a (blank) table with a main label/row for words sharing the same roots and another label/row for words sharing the same patterns in the text such as in the one that follows:

كلمات من نفس الجذر					
ن—ج—ح	←		نَجَحْتُ	نَجاحي	←
د—خ—ل	←		دُخولي	دَخَلْتُ	←
ع—م—ج	←		جمعية	جامِعة	←
ك—و—ن	←	أكون	كان	كانَتْ	←
ر - غ—ب	←		تَرْغَب	رَغْبتي	←
و—ل—د	←		والِدة	والِد	←
ط—ب—ب	←	الأطِبّاء	طَبيبة	الطِّب	←
خ—ر—ج	←		تَخَرُّجي	تَخَرَّجْتُ	←
ح—ص—ل	←		حُصول	حَصَلْتُ	←
كلمات من نفس الوزن					
			دِراسة	تِجارة	←
			حُصول	دُخول	←
			اِنْتِساب	الِتِحاق	←
			حَصَلَ	دَخَلَ	←
			صَديق	طَبيب	←

3. Divide your students into groups of dyads and ask them to identify the words by completing the table (in 10 minutes).
4. Go over your students' responses, for example, by displaying a sample completed table via a document projector and eliciting corrections from all students in class.
5. This activity presupposes knowledge of how to reduce words to their root consonants as well as knowledge of some patterns, but since reducing a word to its root is a skill in and of itself, always review the rules as a whole class.
6. Go over root and pattern meanings.
7. Explain to the class the benefits of this activity in guessing and understanding word meanings and, in turn, helping with comprehending the text.

118 Grammar techniques

Variations

a. Start the activity by identifying some of the words that share the same roots and patterns and elicit students' responses if they are able to guess the meanings of such words from context alone; this should show that relying on the concepts of root and pattern is more robust and more reliable than guessing meanings from context alone.

b. To control for the time spent on the activity, specify the number of words you require your students to find in the text in each of the two categories (e.g., 3–5 each).

6. *Supply the definite article if necessary* أضيفوا الـ التعريف في الفراغ وفق ما يلزم

Purpose

To provide learners with deliberate practice in manipulating definiteness and the rules governing the use of nouns and noun (noun–adjective and *'idāfa*) phrases occurring with or without the definite article. It allows for the integration of deliberate grammar practice with the reading skill. It requires little preparation and takes about 15 minutes to execute.

Procedure

1. Prepare a short, level-appropriate text or select one from your students' textbook, remove all the definite articles, and replace them with blank spaces as in the following sample:

> في هذا ____ فصل، أَسكُن في ____ بَيْت ____ قَديم. ____ بَيْت قريب من ____ جامِعة ____ ميشيغان. فيه ____ غُرفة ____ نوم و ____ غُرفة ____ جُلوس. غُرفة ____ نوم فيها ____ سَرير ____ كَبير و ____ طاولة ____ صَغيرة. ____ طاولة قديمة لكنها جميلة. أُحِبّ ____ قراءة في ____ غُرفة ____ جُلوس بسبب ____ شَمس. أُحِبّ ____ صُفوفي في ____ جامِعة، وأُحِبّ ____ دِراسة ____ لغة ____ عَرَبِيّة لأنّ ____ أُستاذ ____ محمد أُستاذ جَيّد جِدّاً. عِندي ____ صُفوف في أَيّام ____ اِثْنَيْن و ____ ثُلاثاء و ____ أَرْبِعاء . ____ صُفوف تَبْدَأ في ____ ساعة ____ سابعة في ____ صَباح وتنتهي ____ ساعة ____ تاسِعة في ____ مَساء.

2. If you teach case (and mood) endings from this elementary level, and you prefer to make the activity a little challenging, do not provide case endings so you can avoid giving your student additional clues of whether or not a definite article is needed; however, you may want to leave the predicate of verbless sentences without a blank so you can avoid making the activity too challenging, as is demonstrated in the sample text.

Grammar techniques 119

3. Review or go over the definiteness rules briefly where nouns and phrases (whether in the plural or singular and whether concrete or abstract) occur without the definite article if they are introduced in the discourse/text for the first time or if they are proper names and occur otherwise with the definite article (i.e., upon their second mention in the discourse/text, if they are unique nouns, if they are titles, if they involve shared knowledge with readers/interlocuters, or if they refer to entity/entities in general); remind your students also of the special definiteness rule of the 'idāfa phrase, which is marked definite only through the second/last noun of the construction or if that noun is a proper name.
4. Go over any vocabulary items that your students do not know.
5. Distribute copies of the text to your students.
6. Divide your students into dyads and ask them to read the text to each other and write the definite article in the blanks where necessary (in 10 minutes).
7. Go over the sentences as a whole class one sentence at a time by having each group delegate a student to read the sentence aloud to the class and invite students from other groups to provide corrections.
8. Invite your students to ask any questions about the text or the rules involved in the definiteness use.

Variations

a. Instead of using a short text, especially if the text does not cover all or most of the instances of definiteness use, prepare 5–10 short sentences, replacing the definite articles with blank spaces as in the following sample:

١—لا يُحِبُّ أخي ___ لَحْم.
٢—آكُلُ ___ مَوْزة كُلَّ يَوْم.
٣—لا يُحِبّونَ ___ كُرة ___ قَدَم.
٤—هِوايتي ___ سِباحة.
٥—في بَيْتي ___ غُرْفة ___ نَوْم ___ صَغيرة.
٦—كَتَبْتُ ___ واجِب ___ عَرَبِيّة أمْس.
٧—كُلَّ صَباحٍ، أخْرُجُ مِن ___ بَيْت ___ ساعة ___ تاسعة.
٨—___ دكتور ___ جيمس سميث يَسْكُنُ في هذا ___ بَيْت.
٩—___ طَقْس هُنا بارِد جِدّاً في ___ شِتاء.
١٠—لا أُحِبُّ ___ وُصول إلى ___ جامِعة مُتَأخِّراً.

b. Have your students first work individually on the sentences, then divide them into dyads to discuss their responses before going over the sentences as a whole class.

(See Alhawary 2016.)

120   Grammar techniques

7. *Rearranging the scrambled words and making necessary changes* إعادة ترتيب الكلمات المبعثرة مع تغيير ما يلزم

Purpose

To provide learners with deliberate practice in the use of basic sentence structure, including agreement (e.g., verbal and nominal agreement) as well as appropriate pronoun use. It allows for the integration of deliberate grammar practice with the reading and speaking skills. It requires little preparation and takes about 15 minutes to execute.

Procedure

1. Prepare 4–5 typical sentences at your students' level after modifying them slightly, scrambling their word order, and allowing your students to make changes in verbal and nominal agreement and anaphoric pronouns (you may need to leave some words unscrambled so that you allow your students to immediately recognize the appropriate agreement and pronouns involved) such as the following sample sentences:

> 1—واشِنطُن مايكل لي عمّ مَدينة تَسكُنُ اِسْمُها في.
> 2—وَحيد فِعْلًا هي.
> 3—الآن يُدَرِّسُ كاليفورنيا في فاطِمة أَختي جامِعة.
> 4—أَيضاً وَالِدي مُوظَّف وَ مُوظَّف وَالِدتي.
> 5—عُمَر هَذا خالي صُورة.

2. Distribute copies of a handout containing the sentences and ask your students to individually rearrange the words into sentences appropriately while making all necessary changes (in 8 minutes).
3. Divide your students into groups of dyads and have them discuss their reordered sentences and make any changes if they agree with their partners, although they do not always have to agree (in 4 minutes).
4. Go over the sentences as a whole class, with each group reading a sentence and students from other groups providing corrections.

Variations

a. Instead of the groups reading their sentences, divide the board into five columns (and number them accordingly) and have each group delegate a student to go to the board and write one of the sentences.
b. Prepare a teacher's copy of the sentences where the correct sentences are provided underneath their respective scrambled sentences to display on a screen or via a document project to verify students' responses quickly.

Grammar techniques   121

8. *Translate the sentences into Arabic* ترجموا الجمل إلى العربية

Purpose

To provide learners with deliberate practice in the use of one particular grammatical form, such as basic nominal/verbless sentential structure, and serve as a comprehension check of their understating of such a structure and their entailed understanding of phrasal structure (such as noun–adjective and *'idāfa* phrases) and definiteness (i.e., what constitutes a sentence versus a phrase) rules. Thus, the activity is not really about developing translation skills per se. It allows for the integration of deliberate grammar practice with the writing, reading, and speaking skills. It requires little preparation and takes about 25 minutes to execute.

Procedure

1. Using simple vocabulary items (which you can also recycle in subsequent sentences), prepare 5–10 sentences in English to reflect verbless sentences containing demonstrative pronouns, possessive pronouns, proper names, and definite and indefinite noun–adjective and *'idāfa* phrases such as the following sample sentences:

    > 1. This is a tall woman.
    > 2. This woman is tall.
    > 3. This tall woman is in my class.
    > 4. The University of Michigan has many big buildings.
    > 5. This big building has the big library in it.
    > 6. Cairo is an Egyptian city.
    > 7. The picture of the Canadian city is in his house.
    > 8. My office table is very small.
    > 9. There is an office table in this class.
    > 10. The United States of America is a big country.

2. Divide your students into dyads and assign each student to translate five sentences (such as assigning one the first half of the sentences and the other the second half or assigning one the odd numbers and the other the even numbers) and then discuss their sentences together (in 15 minutes).
3. Divide the board into 10 numbered columns (or 5 columns at a time) and have each group delegate a student to write one of the sentences (if there are 10 students in class, each group can write two sentences, with each student writing a sentence).
4. Go over the sentences as a whole group by having each group read their sentence and invite corrections from students of other groups.

122   Grammar techniques

Variations

a. If time is an issue, instead of asking students to write their translated sentences on the board, display students' written translations via a document projector one sentence at a time.
b. Alternatively, if time is not an issue, have groups exchange their written translated sentences and distribute to them a handout of the correct translations beforehand to use as a model in providing corrections and comments to other groups.

(See also Alhawary 2016.)

9. *Sentence parsing* تحديد نوعَي الجمل وتحليلها

Purpose

To provide learners with deliberate practice to parse the two main types of Arabic sentences along with their main constituents by breaking up long or nested sentences that may otherwise be confusing to them or may not enable them to get the full meaning. It allows for the integration of deliberate grammar practice with the reading skill. It requires little preparation and takes 15–20 minutes to execute.

Procedure

1. Find a level-appropriate text of a short paragraph or select one from your students' textbook.
2. Have your students work in groups of dyads to unpack the sentences into short ones by identifying whether a sentence is verbal or verbless, placing a line or forward slash at the end of each sentence, drawing a circle around the verb in verbal sentences, and separating between the two parts of the verbless sentence (المبتدأ "the subject" and الخبر "the predicate") by underlining each part separately (in 10 minutes) as in the following sample:

> أُحِبّ بَيْتي كثيراً /لأنَّهِ كَبير /ولَهُ حَديقة كَبيرة/لكِنْ لا أُحِبّ مَدينَتي/لأنَّ الطَقْس بارد دائماً في الشِّتاء/ ودَرَجَة الرُّطوبَة عاليَة في الصَّيْف /. هذِهِ المَدينَة صَغيرة جِدّاً /لَيْسَ فيها حَدائق عامَة كَثيرة/.
> لي صَديق واحِدَ فَقَط/اِسْمُه عادِل /وهو طالِب في نَفْس الجامعة/ يَدْرُس فيها التّاريخ/.

3. Go over your students' responses as a whole class by having each group delegate a member to read a sentence and identify its type (whether verbal or verbless); if verbless, identify its two parts; if verbal, identify the verb, the subject/doer (and the object/doee if the verb is transitive), and its tense (past or present).
4. Elicit corrections from students of other groups.

Grammar techniques 123

5. Use appropriate language and grammar resources to guide your explanations
and illustrations before and after this activity, since identifying the two parts of
the verbal sentence is based on definiteness use.

(For example, see Alhawary 2011, 2016.)

Variations

a. Repeat this technique often and from early on until students are able to quickly
distinguish between verbal and verbless sentences and identify/look for the subject and object of the verb (in the verbal sentence) and the subject and predicate
(in the verbless sentence).
b. If grammatical endings are taught from early on, teach such endings as part of
the explanation of the verbal and verbless sentence.

10. *Identify the error, if any, and correct it* حدّدوا الخطأ إن وُجد وصحّحوه

Purpose

To provide learners with deliberate practice in the use of a basic construction such
as the noun phrase (i.e., noun–adjective and *'idāfa* phrases) and serve as a comprehension check of their understating of such a structure along with its use with
adjectives, pronouns, and definiteness. The activity allows for the integration of
deliberate grammar practice with, possibly, the speaking skill. It requires little
preparation and takes about 20 minutes to execute.

Procedure

1. Using simple vocabulary, prepare 5–10 sentences in Arabic, some of which contain common errors made by Arabic learners in noun–adjective and *'idāfa* phrases
such as those involving gender, definiteness, possessive pronoun use, word order,
and case endings (if case endings are presented at this level; otherwise, do not
provide sentences with case endings) such as in the following sample sentences:

._____	1——مَدينةُ القاهرةِ مُزْدَحِمةٌ دائماً.
._____	2——هو أُسْتاذٌ مَدْرَسةٍ.
._____	3——تَتَكَلَّمُ صَديقَتي لُغَةَ الإسْبانيَّةِ.
._____	4——أَسْكُنُ في الوِلايَةِ فيرجينيا.
._____	5——غُرْفَتي نَوْمٍ صَغيرةٌ.

124 Grammar techniques

> 6—نُحِبُّ مُدَرِّسينَ المَدْرَسةِ. _____ .
>
> 7—يَدْرُسُ صَديقي مُصْطَفَى لِلتَّخَصُّصِ في الشَّرْقِ الأَوْسَطِ سياسَةٍ. _____
>
> _____ .
>
> 8—لا نُحِبُّ الازْدِحامَ في الشَّوارعِ المَدينةِ. _____ .
>
> 9—هو والدُ صَديقِهِ القَديمِ جيفري. _____ .
>
> 10—زَوْجَةُ أُستاذِنا جَديدٍ طَبيبةٌ. _____ .

2. A few of the sentences (e.g., 1 and 9) should be error-free so that your students are also able to recognize correct grammatical structures, that they do not assume automatically all sentences contain errors, and that they give the activity their full attention in activating their grammatical rule application abilities; be sure to tell your students that not all sentences contain errors.
3. Ask your students to individually read the sentences and identify the errors by underlining them or drawing a circle around them (in 5 minutes).
4. Divide your students into dyads and ask them to collaborate in correcting the errors by writing the corrections above the errors or to the left of the sentence; instruct your students not to copy the entire sentence in fixing the errors (8 minutes).
5. Go over the sentences as a whole class one sentence at a time by having each group delegate a student to read the sentence aloud to the class and (a) confirm whether a sentence is grammatically accurate, (b) identify the errors if the sentence is not grammatically accurate, and (c) suggest corrections.
6. Invite students from other groups to help with any of the three (a–c) required actions.
7. Invite students to ask any questions related to the sentences or target structures of this activity.

Variations

a. Other grammatical points can be the target of this activity, such as verbal agreement (between the subject and the verb), gender and number agreement (between the noun and attributive adjective or between the subject and predicate of the nominal/verbless sentence), and mood endings (on verbs) if presented at this level.
b. For the sentences that are error-free, ask your students to introduce an error or errors that they would usually make.

(See also Alhawary 2016.)

2. Developing grammatical competence at the intermediate level

While techniques for developing the four language skills and entailed functional abilities are essential for developing communicative competence within the communicative language teaching approach, techniques aimed to provide deliberate and purposeful practice for developing grammatical competence are equally important.

Grammar techniques included in the intermediate level continue to focus on basic grammatical structures at the word, phrase, and sentence levels. It is important whenever possible to integrate grammar techniques with those intended for developing language skills. Doing so has many added benefits, including driving boredom out of the teaching of grammar, demonstrating to learners the important role of grammar in carrying meanings, and optimizing classroom time by also developing other skills.

11. Using the imperative and negative imperative استخدام صيغتَي الأمر والنهي

Purpose

To provide learners with deliberate practice in the use of the imperative and negative imperative constructions. It allows for the integration of deliberate grammar practice with possibly the speaking and writing skills. The activity is best used after students are presented with the rules of the imperative in the different verb forms (I–VIII and X) and different persons (second-person singular, dual, and plural for both genders). It requires little preparation and takes about 15–20 minutes to execute.

Procedure

1. Provide pictures of different persons (one male, one female, two males, two females, three males, and three females) doing various activities, such as eating drinking, writing, reading, teaching, helping, traveling, cooking/preparing, talking (on the phone), sleeping, walking, buying, giving, smoking, burning, etc.).
2. Add a check mark to the picture to indicate the verb to be formed should be in the imperative and an "X" for the verb to be formed in the negative imperative.
3. Display the pictures one at a time on the board, screen, or via a document projector.
4. Ask one student at a time in a chain fashion to form the imperative or negative imperative inflected for the proper person as indicated next to the picture.
5. If a student is not able to form the correct verb (in the imperative or negative imperative), skip them and go to the next student, skip that student to the next one, and so on until a student forms the correct verb.
6. For the next picture/verb, start with the student who could not form the previous verb and repeat the preceding step.
7. If all students could not figure out a certain verb, offer students some clues or model for them a verb of the same pattern and elicit the correct form of the verb in question.

Variations

a. If finding pictures for use in the dual and the plural is difficult, prepare pictures for at least a male and a female person and make three duplicate copies of each and add to each the number 1, 2, or 3, signifying singular, dual, and plural, respectively.

126 Grammar techniques

b. Divide students into groups of 3 and distribute to each 3–6 pictures (1–2 per student) and allow them to write the imperative and/or negative imperfective relevant to the pictures they have (3–6 minutes).

c. Upon displaying a picture, ask the group who has the identical picture to produce (aloud) the imperative or negative imperative.

d. Elicit corrections from students in other groups.

e. The activity can use both sound and weak verbs, but preferably when first implemented, the activity is better employed with sound verbs alone and later with weak (and sound) verbs.

12. Find your classmates according to their actions ابحثوا عن زملائكم وفق أفعالهم

Purpose

To provide learners with deliberate practice in the use of verb tenses, especially past, present, and future tenses, and their negation forms. It allows for the integration of deliberate grammar practice with the writing, listening, and speaking skills. It requires little preparation and takes about 20 minutes to execute.

Procedure

1. Using index cards or sheets of paper, prepare three sets of questions (one for the past tense, another for the present tense, and a third for the future tense), with each set consisting of 3–5 questions for your students to use in asking their classmates, such as "who traveled to a foreign country" for the past tense, "who plays tennis" for the present tense, and "who will travel to a foreign country this summer" for the future tense, as in the following samples:

> ابحثوا عن زملائكم:
> 1——من منهم سافر إلى بلد أجنبي؟
> 2——من منهم قرأ كتاب ألف ليلة وليلة؟
> 3——من منهم قابل شخصية مشهورة؟

> ابحثوا عن زملائكم:
> 1——من منهم يلعب التنس؟
> 2——من منهم يدرس في البيت؟
> 3——من منهم يعمل في مكتبة الجامعة؟

> ابحثوا عن زملائكم:
> 1——من منهم سيسكن مع أسرته في الصيف القادم؟
> 2——من منهم سيسافر إلى بلد أجنبي في الصيف القادم؟
> 3——من منهم سيقرأ كتاب ألف ليلة وليلة في الصيف القادم؟

Grammar techniques 127

2. Make duplicate copies of the cards/sheets to reflect the number of your students in class so that if you have 12 students, you need to have 4 copies of each and so on.
3. Divide your students into groups of 3 and give each student a different set of questions.
4. Ask students within each group to take turns in asking each other the questions they have.
5. Instruct your students that they are to ask each other, using direct questions such as هل سافرتَ/سافرتِ إلى بلد أجنبي؟ "Did you travel to a foreign country," and that they are to write down the answer to each question in a complete sentence whether the answer is in the affirmative (e.g., جون سافر إلى المغرب "John traveled to Morocco") or in the negative (e.g., جون لم يسافر إلى بلد أجنبي "John did not travel to a foreign country").
6. Go over your students' responses as a whole class, with each student reporting on what they found out about the other two members of the group.
7. Elicit corrections from students of other groups.
8. Reinforce the grammatical points related to tense and negation by writing the common errors on the board with an additional explanation or a brief review of the rules.

Variations

a. Distribute the three sets of questions to your students one for each, evenly if possible.
b. Instruct your students to go around individually and ask at least three other students randomly.
c. Go over sample responses, 1–2 samples of each of the three sets of questions.
d. Other Arabic tenses and their negation forms (for an exhaustive list and explanation of Arabic tenses, see Alhawary 2011), adverbs, or negation of the verbless sentence can be practiced by implementing the same technique.

(See also Ur 2009.)

13. *Compare yourselves* قارنوا بين أنفسكم

Purpose

To provide learners with deliberate practice in using the أفعل pattern to express the comparative and superlative degrees of adjectives derived from triliteral form I verbs. It allows for the integration of deliberate grammar practice with the speaking and possibly writing skills. The activity is best implemented after students are presented with the أفعل pattern rules. It requires little preparation and takes about 20–25 minutes to execute.

128 Grammar techniques

Procedure

1. Prepare a list of adjectives derived from triliteral form I verbs as many as there are students, with one adjective on a separate index card/sheet of paper, many of which should pertain to obvious physical attributes as much as possible and avoid negatively perceived attributes such as in the following list:

طَويل
قَصير
كبير
صَغير
نَحيف
خَفيف
كَريم
سَريع
قَويّ
غَنيّ

2. Divide your students into groups of 3 and distribute three cards to each group.
3. Ask members in each group to compare themselves with each other with respect to the three adjectives that they received in the cards, with a total of nine sentences (in 6–9 minutes); for example, in the group that received the card containing the adjective **طَويل** "tall," one member is tall or not tall → إليزابيث طَويلة/غير طَويلة; another member is taller than another → جيمس أطول من إليزابيث, and a third member is the tallest → جوليا أطول الطلاب/طالبة
4. Ask each group to prepare/write three sets of three statements, using one adjective in each set of three statements.
5. Go over your students' responses as a whole class, with each group member reporting to the class a set of three statements pertaining to one adjective comparing the three group members, with each group reporting a total of nine statements.
6. Elicit corrections from students of other groups.
7. Invite your students to ask questions about this structure and related ones.

Variations

a. Provide copies of the entire list to each student and ask each group to select three adjectives from the list.
b. Divide groups to consist of only males or only females so that the full range of gender use with the structure can be practiced and can be more evident.
c. Have a group exchange their statements with at least another group for corrections and comments.
d. Allow time for each group to incorporate the comments and corrections.

Grammar techniques 129

14. Using the passive voice استخدام الفعل المبني للمجهول

Purpose

To provide learners with deliberate practice in using the active and passive voice constructions. It allows for the integration of deliberate grammar practice with the writing, reading, and speaking skills. The activity is best implemented after students are presented with the rules of passive voice derivation in the different verb forms (in particular, I–VI, VIII, and X). It requires little preparation and takes about 15–20 minutes to execute.

Procedure

1. Prepare index cards/sheets of paper, each containing an 'idāfa phrase with the first noun being a verbal noun such as استخدام الماء "the use of water" so your students can form a meaningful sentence in the active voice (containing minimally a subject/ doer, a verb, and object/doee) as in يَستَخدِمُ النـاسُ المـاءَ كلَّ يوم "People use water every day" and another in the passive as in يُستَخدَمُ الماءُ كلَّ يوم "Water is used every day"; the instances of the verbal nouns used should reflect the different verb forms used in the passive voice (i.e., forms I–VI, VIII, and X), with preferably all belonging to sound verbs when this activity is used for the first time, as in the following list:

> كتابة الرسائل
>
> تعليم اللغات الأجنبية
>
> مساعدة الناس
>
> إكرام الضَّيف
>
> تقبّل العمل
>
> مقابلة المدير
>
> اختراع الهاتف الذكي
>
> استخدام الحاسوب

2. Distribute 1–2 cards/sheets to each student and instruct them to individually make up a sentence out of the phrase (consisting minimally of a subject/doer, a verb, and an object/doee) in the active voice and to write it down on the card/ sheet of paper; the verb form to be used should match that of the verbal noun given in the phrase (in 2–4 minutes).
3. Divide your students into dyads and ask your students to exchange the cards/ sheets with their partners and write/transform the sentence into passive voice, paying attention to what needs to be deleted and the change in grammatical endings, and discuss them with each other (in 4–6 minutes).
4. Go over your students' sentences as a whole class, by first having dyads write their sentences on the board (or displaying them via the document projector) and reading their sentences out to the class.
5. Elicit corrections from other students in other groups.

130 Grammar techniques

Variations

a. Either as a follow-up activity or within the same activity, include instances of assimilated, hollow, and defective verbal nouns so students can practice deriving passive voice of such forms.

b. Ask each student to add/make up their own sentence in the passive voice to share with the class.

15. *Nominal sentence parsing* تحديد الجمل الاسمية وتمييز رُكنَيها مع الإعراب

Purpose

To provide learners with deliberate practice to parse Arabic nominal sentences along with their two constituent parts occurring with *'inna* and its sisters and *kāna* and its sisters together with their grammatical (case) endings. It allows for the integration of deliberate grammar practice with the reading skill. It requires little to no preparation and takes about 30–35 minutes to execute.

Procedure

1. Prepare a level-appropriate text of interest or relevant to your students or use one from your students' textbook, containing nominal sentences occurring with and without *'inna* and its sisters and *kāna* and its sisters, such as in the following text (from Hanan Al-Sheikh's novel *My Story is a Long Explanation*) without case endings:

أغادر البلد /وأنا مصعوقةٌ، مملوءةٌ بالغضبِ/لأنَّ المسلمينَ و المسيحيّينَ يتقاتلون/و لأنَّ من بين الجثثِ عند الجسر بائعي الصحفِ من الأولاد الصغار. /والذي حزَّ بقلبي ذهابي إلى المصيف نفسه/فنزور كلّنا صديقتي/فأطمئنَ عليها وعلى عائلتها /وإذا بابنها الذي كنتُ أمازحه قبل أشهر يطرد زوج ابنتي /لأنَّهُ فلسطينيٌّ/فأعضُّ على إصبعي لأصدّق/أنَّ ما يحدثُ هو واقعٌ /ولَيْسَ وهماً /. . . أكتشف /وأنا بعيدةٌ عن أجواءِ الحربِ/- سرّ ضياعي بدل فرحتي./فأنا قد اعتدت على أن /أكونَ ضمنَ مجموعةٍ/ وأن/أكونَ لولبَ الجلسةِ. /رحلتي الأولى كانَتْ إلى الكويتِ /وهناك تقتل الكويت نفسيّتي بقسوة. طقسها، وعدم تأقلمي معه/ ولا ينشرح صدري إلّا حين تهبّ الرياح ذات مساء /فأفتح زجاج النافذة حتّى أتنفّس الهواء الطبيعيّ لا هواء المكيّف/لكنّي أنهضُ في الصَّباح . . . /وكأنّي سمكةٌ/غطَّسَتْ بالطحين /وتركتُ قبل أن ترمى في المقلي./ ولمّا لم نجلس على الشرفات/ شعرت /وكأنّ بيتَ ابنتي الجميلَ لَيْسَ إلّا سجناً./ أعدّ أصناف الطعام من أجل /أن يدعو زوج ابنتي زملاءه في العمل./ أتحمّس بادئ الأمر لمهمّتي الجديدة /وكُلّي تمنٍّ .../قد أصبحتُ أمّاً وجدّةً مثاليَّةً.

---

2. Draw your students' attention (initially) to the presence of *'inna* and *kāna* or any of their sisters by marking them such as placing them in bold.

Grammar techniques 131

3. Have your students work in groups of dyads to unpack the text (consisting of no fewer than 32 sentences) into short ones by identifying whether a sentence is verbal or nominal, placing a line or forward slash at the end of each sentence, and indicating the two parts of the nominal sentence (المبتدأ "the subject" and الخبر "the predicate") by underlining the subject (whether a noun or a pronoun) and placing a double underline under the predicate, whether or not preceded by *'inna* and and *kāna* and their sisters (in 10–12 minutes).
4. Go over your students' responses as a whole class by having each group delegate a member to read a nominal sentence (leaving verbal sentences identified but not the target of this main activity).
5. Elicit corrections from students of other groups.
6. Redivide your students into new dyads and have them work on the case endings of the subjects and predicates, observing the rules of accusative markings of the subject and predicate occurring without or with *'inna* and its sisters versus *kāna* and its sisters and when the verb occurs as a predicate (i.e., following its own rules of mood marking) as well as the occurrence of a word both as a predicate to a preceding subject and a subject to a following predicate (which occurs twice in the above sample text as indicated in the double non-straight lines; in 8–10 minutes).
7. Go over your students' responses as a whole class by having each group delegate a member to read a nominal sentence fully vocalized.
8. Elicit corrections from students of other groups.
9. It is fine to skip a related grammatical form in the text that is above your students' level.

Variations

a. Repeat this technique until students are able to quickly distinguish between verbal and nominal sentences and their constituent parts.
b. As a follow-up activity, and following the same procedure, have your students work on identifying the subject/doer, verb, and object/doee of each of the verbal sentences.
c. A table consisting of 3 columns such as the following one can be used in which students are asked to write the different constituent parts of each of the nominal sentences found in the text (see also Alhawary 2016):

الخبر	المبتدأ	إنّ/كانَ/ . . .

16. *Provide your reasons* عَلِّلوا أسبابكم

Purpose

To provide learners with deliberate practice in constructing complex sentences with embedded clauses, especially with the complementizer لأنّ "because" used to

132 Grammar techniques

provide elaborations or reasoning. It allows for the integration of deliberate grammar practice possibly with the writing and speaking skills. It requires little preparation and takes about 20 minutes to execute.

Procedure

1. Prepare a list of 10–20 everyday items, such as حاسوب "computer," ساعة "watch," درّاجة "bicycle," سيّارة "car," تلفاز "television," مذياع/راديو "radio," نظّارات شمسية "sunglasses," عطر "perfume," ملابس "clothes," حذاء "shoes."
2. Distribute copies or display the list on the board, screen, or via a document projector.
3. Arrange your students' seats in a semicircle.
4. Ask each student to choose two items, one that they "need" and another that they "do not need," and provide a valid reason why in one long sentence in each case, with one student making one statement at a time in a chain fashion.
5. Provide correction by means of recasting, elicit corrections from other students, or take notes of relevant errors and work on them as a whole class at the end of the activity.

Variations

a. Instead of items of words, provide pictures on index cards of famous personalities, different types of foods, vegetables or fruits, different places, different universities, and so on.
b. Have each student pick a picture of an object or person that they "like" and another they "do not like" or "prefer" and do "not prefer" and provide a reason why in one long sentence in each case.
c. Have students rehearse their sentences in groups of dyads before working on the sentences as a whole class.

17. *Collapse into one sentence* ادمجوا كل جملتين في جملة واحدة

Purpose

To provide learners with deliberate practice in constructing complex sentences with embedded clauses, using relative pronouns that are inflected for gender and number. It allows for the integration of deliberate grammar practice possibly with the writing, reading, and speaking skills. It requires little preparation and takes about 20 minutes to execute.

Procedure

1. Prepare 5–10 pairs of sentences that can be collapsed into one by using a relative pronoun if necessary (i.e., only when the modified noun/noun phrase is definite)

Grammar techniques   133

and making any necessary changes such as eliminating redundant words such as in the following sample sentences:

> ‏1—وصلتْ مديرة المكتب. تعمل مديرة المكتب هنا.
> ‏2—وصل القطار. ينقل القطار الرّكّاب القادمين من مدينة طنجة.
> ‏3—قابلتُ الطالبيَن. جاء الطالبان إلى المكتبة في الأسبوع الماضي.
> ‏4—لي قريبة. تسكن قريبتي مع زوجها في مدينة الدوحة في قطر.
> ‏5—جاء أصدقاء والدي إلى بيتنا أمس. يعمل أصدقاء والدي في الوزارة.
> ‏6—فازتْ طالبتان بالمسابقة. تدرس الطالبتان في جامعتنا.
> ‏7—اشتريتُ كتاب أستاذك. كتاب أستاذك يعجبك كثيراً.
> ‏8—سلّمتُ على النساء. تُحضر النساء أولادهن للعب في الحديقة العامة كل يوم.
> ‏9—عند صديقتي سيّارة جديدة. لون سيّارة صديقتي الجديدة أحمر.
> ‏10—حكى الأستاذ لنا قصة غريبة. حدثتْ القصة الغريبة لأستاذنا في فرنسا.

2. Explain to your students (by way of providing the first pair of sentences as an example) that they are to combine each pair of sentences into one, using a connector if necessary, and making any other necessary changes so that the first pair of sentences would be reworded as ‏وصلت مديرة المكتب التي تعمل هنا "The office manager who works here arrived."

3. Divide your students into groups of 3 and have each student within a group work on 1–3 pairs of sentences and then discuss them with their partners (in 10 minutes).

4. Go over your students' newly constructed sentences as a group, with each group delegating a student to read a sentence until all groups have shared at least one sentence with the class.

5. Elicit corrections from students of other groups.

Variations

a. Ask each group (of 3) to work on only three pairs of sentences and write them on an index card/sheet of paper and exchange them with another group for corrections.

b. Allow enough time for groups to make corrections to their sentences before working on all the sentences as a whole class.

(See Alhawary 2016.)

18.   Name the structure in the text   ‏سمّوا التركيب في النصّ

Purpose

To provide learners with deliberate practice in the use of one particular grammatical structure (and relevant subtypes) in context. It allows for the integration of deliberate

134 Grammar techniques

grammar practice with the reading and (possibly) speaking skills. It requires little preparation and takes about 20–25 minutes to execute.

Procedure

1. Prepare a level-appropriate text or select one from your students' textbook or from Alhawary (2016) on a particular grammatical structure such as التَّمييز "adverb of specification" and mark all instances of the structure (e.g., by underlining, bolding highlighting, or drawing a circle around them) as in the following text (excerpted from Abdulhakim Qasim's short novel *Al-Mahdi*):

> المَوْكِبُ يَقْتَرِبُ مِنَ الجَامِعِ، يَزْدادُ الصُّراخُ مِنْ مُكَبِّراتِ الصَّوْتِ اِنْفِعالًا، تَزْدادُ قَرْعاتُ الطُّبولِ عُنْفاً، يَزْدادُ وَقْعُ أَقْدامِ الجَوّالَةِ في الأَحْذِيَةِ الرَّثَّةِ حَماساً، والنّاسُ المُحيطونَ بِالمُعَلِّمِ يَزْدادونَ كَثافَةً وجُنوناً، وعاصِفَةُ الغُبارِ تَزْدادُ كَثافَةً، والشَّمْسُ تَدُقُّ مَساميرَ مُحَماةً بِالنّارِ في جَبينِ المُعَلِّمِ. يَتَرَنَّحُ على الفَرَسِ، وإذْ يُنْزِلونَهُ عِنْدَ بابِ المَسْجِدِ يَنْكَفِئُ على وَجْهِهِ فاقِدَ الوَعْيِ "لَقَدْ ماتَ المَهْدي" تَماماً. وكالنّارِ في الهَشيمِ تَنْطَلِقُ في النّاسِ صَرْخَةٌ والنّاسُ حَوْلَهُ يُجْلِسونَهُ على الأَرْضِ يَهُزّونَهُ ويَرْبِتونَ على صُدْغَيْهِ دونَ جَدْوَى.

2. Provide copies of the text or display it on the screen or via a document projector.
3. Ask your students to read the text and name the underlined grammatical structure individually or in groups of two and what grammatical features distinguish it as such (in 10 minutes).
4. Go over your students' responses as a whole class by having each student read a sentence in a chain fashion; if the sentence contains an underlined word, have the student name the grammatical structure and the features that distinguish it as such (i.e., in this case, being singular, indefinite, mostly as a non-derived noun, with the accusative case ending, and is used to clarify the meaning of the verb or the verbless sentence with which it occurs in term of quality, quantity, etc.).
5. Elicit corrections from all students in the class.
6. Invite questions from your students about the structure and similar ones (such as other types of adverbs that may be confused with adverbs of specification).

Variations

a. Instead of providing all instances of the target structure marked in the text, remove all such markings and ask your students to find all 6 or 5–6 instances of the structure, in this case, adverb of specification.
b. To make the activity a little more challenging, remove all case (and mood) endings and ask your students to supply case endings on all instances of adverb of specification after identifying them.

(See Alhawary 2016.)

Grammar techniques   135

19. *Translate into Arabic* ترجموا إلى العربية

Purpose

To provide learners with deliberate practice in reviewing a number of grammatical structures learners have learned thus far and to serve as a comprehension check of their understating of such structures and related grammatical points. Thus, the activity is not really about developing translation skills per se. It allows for the integration of deliberate grammar practice with, possibly, the writing, reading, and speaking skills. It requires little preparation and takes about 20–25 minutes to execute.

Procedure

1. Using simple vocabulary items, prepare 5–10 sentences in English to reflect a selected number of grammatical structures that your students have covered in class thus far and that you would like to use this activity as a review of such structures (e.g., indefinite-definite *'idāfa* phrase where the first noun is indefinite and the second/last definite, tenses such as the present perfect and future perfect, adverbs of manner, the number phrase, and conditional sentences) such as in the following sample sentences:

   1. I work in a new Ford office.
   2. We drink coffee in a State Street café.
   3. The president has just arrived in Paris.
   4. By 2025, they will have lived in Detroit for 50 years.
   5. They came to me, asking for help.
   6. He always comes late to class.
   7. She has three houses and twelve cars.
   8. Our university has forty thousand students, twenty-five buildings, and eight libraries.
   9. If you work hard, you will get what you want.
   10. If I had traveled to Japan, I would have gone to mount Fuji.

2. Divide your students into dyads and assign each student to translate five sentences (such as assigning one the first half of the sentences and the other the second half or assigning one the odd numbers and the other the even numbers) and then discuss their sentences together (in 15 minutes).
3. Divide the board into 10 numbered columns (or 5 columns at a time) and have each group delegate a student to write one of the sentences (if there are 10 students in class, each group can write two sentences, with each student writing a sentence).
4. Go over the sentences as a whole group by group by having each group read their sentence and then inviting corrections from students of other groups.
5. Invite your students to ask any questions about the structures and related ones.

136 Grammar techniques

Variations

a. If time is an issue, instead of asking students to write their translated sentences on the board, display students' written translations via a document projector one sentence at a time.

b. Alternatively, if time is not an issue, have groups exchange their written translated sentences and distribute to them a handout of the correct translated sentences beforehand to use as a model in providing correction comments on the translations of other groups.

(See also Alhawary 2016.)

20. *Identify the errors, if any, and correct them* حدّدوا الأخطاء إن وُجدت وصحّحوها

Purpose

To provide learners with deliberate practice in the use of a number of grammatical structures learners have covered thus far and to serve as a comprehension check of their understating of such structures and related grammatical points. The activity allows for the integration of deliberate grammar practice with possibly the speaking skill. It requires little preparation and takes about 20–25 minutes to execute.

Procedure

1. Using simple vocabulary, prepare 5–10 sentences in Arabic, some of which contain common errors made by Arabic learners in a number of grammatical structures that your students have covered thus far, such as those related to verbal agreement forms, case and mood endings, subtle uses of definiteness (such as indefinite subjects), the number phrase, defective nouns, the five nouns, and conditional sentences such as in the following sample sentences:

1—هذِهِ الطّالباتُ لا تَكْتُبْنَ الواجِبَ. _____ .

2—ماتَ في الحادثِ أكثرَ من عشرةِ أشخاصٍ. _____ .

3—يُريدونَ أنْ يُسافرونَ إلى مدينةِ الجزائرِ. _____ .

4—رجلٌ دَخَلَ علينا وبدأ يتكلَّم بالفرنسيّةِ. _____ .

5—مدرسةٌ قديمةٌ أفضلُ من حديقةٍ جميلةٍ. _____ .

6—الْتَحَقَ خمسُ طالباتٍ سورياتٍ بالجامعةِ. _____ .

7—بدأ والدهُ يُعامِلُهُ بحكمةٍ أكثرَ فهو الآنَ في الثامنةِ عَشْرَةِ من عمرِهِ. _____

_____ .

8—بعد أن دخلتُ الغرفةَ دَخَلَ مُحامٍ وسلَّمَ عَليَّ. _____ .

9—حَضَرَ أخي إلى الحفلةِ ولكنَّ أخُ صَديقي لم يَحضُرْ. _____ .

10—لو كنتُ مكانَك فسأُدرسُ في هذه الجامعةِ. _____ .

Grammar techniques 137

2. A few of the sentences (5 and 6) should be error-free so that your students are also able to recognize correct grammatical structures, that they do not assume automatically all sentences contain errors, and that they give the activity their full attention in activating their grammatical rule application abilities; be sure to tell your students that not all sentences contain errors.
3. Ask your students to individually read the sentences and identify the errors by underlining them or drawing a circle around them (in 10 minutes).
4. Divide your students into dyads and ask them to collaborate in correcting the errors by writing the corrections above the errors or to the left of the sentence; instruct your students not to copy the entire sentence in fixing the errors (5–7 minutes).
5. Go over the sentences as a whole class one sentence at a time by having each group delegate a student to read a sentence aloud to the class and (a) confirm whether the sentence is grammatically correct, (b) identify the errors if the sentence is not grammatically correct, and (c) suggest corrections.
6. Invite students from other groups to help with any of the three (a–c) required actions.
7. Invite students to ask any questions related to the structures and related ones.

Variations

a. Other grammatical points can be the target of this activity as needed and as covered in class.
b. For the 1–2 sentences that are error-free, ask your students to introduce an error or errors that they would usually make.

(See also Alhawary 2016.)

3. Developing grammatical competence at the advanced level

While techniques for developing the four language skills and entailed functional abilities are essential for developing communicative competence within the communicative language teaching approach, techniques aimed to provide deliberate and purposeful practice for developing grammatical competence are equally important. Grammar techniques included in the advanced level focus on less basic and more complex grammatical structures than those in the previous intermediate level. It is important whenever possible to integrate grammar techniques with those developing language skills. Doing so has many added benefits including driving boredom out of the teaching of grammar, demonstrating to learners the important role of grammar in carrying meanings, and optimizing classroom time by also developing other skills.

21. *Dictogloss of a grammar point* "إملاء "الديكتوغلوس لنصّ يحتوي على تركيب معيّن

Purpose

To provide learners with deliberate practice in the use of a particular grammatical structure and their ability to recognize such a structure as well as recall the

138 Grammar techniques

application of the relevant rules. The activity allows for the integration of deliberate grammar practice with the listening, speaking, reading, and writing skills. It requires little preparation and takes about 20–25 minutes to execute.

Procedure

1. Prepare a level-appropriate text or select (about 50 words) one from your students' textbook or from Alhawary (2016) containing instances of a particular grammatical structure such as exclamation as in the following text extracted from *The Arabian Nights*:

> وأَدْرَكَ شَهْرَزادَ الصَّباحِ، فَسَكَتَتْ عَنِ الكَلامِ المُباحِ. فقالَتْ لَها أُخْتُها دُنيا زاد:
> يا أُخْتي، ما أَحْلَى حَديثَكِ وأَطْيَبَهُ وأَلَذَّهُ وأَعْذَبَهُ! فقالَت شَهْرَزاد: وأينَ هذا مِمّا
> سأُحَدِّثُكُم بِه اللَّيْلَةَ المُقْبِلَةَ إنْ عِشْتُ وأَبْقاني المَلِكُ. فقالَ المَلِكُ: واللهِ لا أَقْتُلُها حَتّى
> أَسْمَعَ حَديثَها لأَنَّهُ عَجيب . . .

2. Read the text once to your student at normal speed.
3. Allow your students to take notes.
4. Divide your students into groups of 3 (the more students, the easier the task will be) and ask them to reconstruct the text with all grammatical case (and mood) endings based on what they have just heard and their written notes (in 8 minutes, 2 minutes per sentence).
5. Collapse two groups into one group and allow your students one more chance to reconstruct the text along with case and mood endings (in about 8 minutes).
6. Go over your students' responses by having each group present their text by delegating a student to read it while preferably displaying it to the class via a document projector.
7. Invite your students to ask questions about the target structure and related ones.

Variations

a. Instead of collapsing each two groups into one, distribute copies of the written text without supplying case (and mood) endings.
b. Other grammatical structures can be the target of this activity, such as the number phrase, conditional sentences, the exceptive phrase, the apposition phrase, and the diptote.

(For texts of different structures, see Alhawary 2011.)

22. *Complete the speculations* أكملوا التكهّنات

Purpose

To provide deliberate practice in the use of conditional sentences, in particular the three types: the possible/probable by using particles such as إذا "if" and إنْ "if," the improbable by using لو "if" or لولا "where it not for," and the impossible by using لو "if/had." It allows for the integration of deliberate grammar practice with the speaking or writing skill. It requires little to no preparation and takes about 15–20 minutes to execute.

Procedure

1. Go over the meaning and rules of forming the type of conditional sentence that you want to provide your students with deliberate practice in, such as the improbable sentence involving the use of لو "if."
2. Explain to your students that each one is to use the second part of the conditional sentence constructed by a previous student as their first part.
3. Arrange the seats in class in a semicircle (or two semicircles one behind the other, depending on the number of students).
4. Stand or sit where the right end of the semicircle is to your right and the left end to your left.
5. Turn to the student to your right or left; if turning to the student to your right, model the conditional sentence by stating لو أنا غنيّ، لكنت في طوكيو الآن "If I were rich, I would be in Tokyo now."
6. Using the second part of your sentence as their part, that student should respond with a sentence such as لو أنا في طوكيو الآن لذهبت إلى مطعم سوشي "If I were in Tokyo now, I would go to a sushi restaurant."
7. The next student should use the second part of the conditional sentence as their first part and so on.
8. The chain of speculations about students' wishes continues in the same fashion until each student in the class has constructed a conditional sentence of the same type, recycling the second part of the sentence of a previous student.
9. Reinforce the rules involved by writing 2–3 conditional sentences (or having some students write the sentences they have produced) on the board, inviting any questions your students may have, and correcting errors that students may have produced during the activity.

Variations

a. A series of pictures (presented on slides/screen or via a document projector) of different activities or locations can be presented for students to use in their second part of the conditional sentence.
b. Index cards or sheets of paper can be used containing the first part of one of the types of the conditional sentences that students can select (1–3 each) randomly (such as ماذا ستفعل إذا/إن تخرّجت هذه السنة؟ "What will you do if you graduate this year?," ماذا كنت تفعل لو (كان) عندك مليون دولار "What would you do if you had a million dollars?," and ماذا كنت تفعل لو سافرت إلى سورية السنة الماضية؟ "What would you have done if you had traveled to Syria last year?") and then ask the student next to them in the chain one question at a time.

140   Grammar techniques

c. Instead of constructing the conditional sentences verbally, have students write their sentences on a sheet of paper to be passed from one student to another.
d. Display the written sentence on the board or via a document projector and go over the chain of sentences as a whole class, inviting corrections from everyone.

(See also Ur 2009.)

23. *Identify your errors and correct them* حدّدوا أخطاءكم وصحّحوها

Purpose

To provide learners with deliberate practice in the use of grammatical structures that they have learned but are still making errors in producing them in their classroom speech and writing assignments. Instead of providing direct or indirect error corrections during communicative activities, addressing error corrections during this activity allows learners to engage in communicative activities freely without being interrupted by the teacher, which may otherwise hinder their development of speaking fluency and/or disrupt the pace of communicative activities in which they engage. The activity allows for the integration of deliberate grammar practice with the speaking skill. It requires little preparation and takes about 25 minutes to execute.

Procedure

1. On a biweekly (or as often as needed) basis, prepare a list of 10–30 common or frequent errors that your students have been making during communicative (speaking) activities and in their writing assignments; such a list can be arranged in a table and contain purely grammatical errors, errors due to wrong choice of word (nominal, verbal, adjectival) patterns, errors due to the wrong selection or absence of a preposition, and errors related to style such as the sample of errors in the following table:

أخطاء في الأسلوب	أخطاء في الأوزان أو حروف الجر	الأخطاء النحْوية	
توقعاته ليست الواقع	لا شيء قد غيَّر	الأقوى بلاد ستسيطر على الآخرين	1-
مــن طبقــة اجتمـاعـي الموظفين	يحدِّثون عن أشياء	لا تشجع الناس الطيبون	2-

لا تشجع الناس الطيبين	يهتمون عن العمل	يعرف المواطنون أنّ قادتهم ليس معصوم عن الخطأ	3-
مِثلَ قال أريد . . .	أوافق مع الكاتب	الحياة ليس عادلة	4-
عنده الذكريات عن بداية عمله	أوافق مع هذا الكلام	معظم المـوظفـون غير طيبون	5-
بعض من الناس يقولون إن ليس في مكان للدين في الدولة المدنية	أثَّرت بأسلوب الكاتب	يعتقد أن هذا الظلم.	6-
يؤثر على العائلة بليغاً	يريد أن يزوّج	عنده الذكريات عن بداية عمله	7-
يطلبون حقوقهم وحرياتهم	عندما يصل في العمل	ليس كانَ عندهم وحدة	8-
تعرّفت على الشاب من تزوّج صديقتي	سيشعرون راحة كثيرة	يجعله أن يمثل دور الأب	9-
لـم يـجـد فـي الـتـاريـخ الإسلامي هذا المفهوم	الدّول العربية عندها عدد كبير من الباحثين	يـجـب أن الأم والأب يعملون	10-

2. Inform your students that these are their own errors that they have made recently either in speaking activities in class or in their writing assignments.
3. Divide your students into dyads and ask them to collaborate in identifying and correcting their errors one error type/column at a time (5 minutes per column).
4. Go over the errors as a whole class one error at a time by having each group delegate a member to identify the error and suggest a correction.
5. Elicit corrections from students of other groups if a group is not able to identify the error or provide a proper correction.
6. Invite students to ask any questions about the structures and related ones.

Variations

a. Allow groups 2 additional minutes after the time of each error type expires to ask other groups about an error they could not identify or could not correct.
b. Have students initially work individually on each error type/column (5 minutes per column) before dividing them into dyads to discuss their answers (in 5 minutes), but this will take more time for the activity to be completed.

142 Grammar techniques

24. *Compare your attributes* قارنوا بين خِصالكم

Purpose

To provide learners with deliberate practice in using التمييز "adverbs of specification" to express the comparative and superlative degrees. It allows for the integration of deliberate grammar practice with the speaking and possibly writing skills. The activity is best implemented after students are presented with the rules of adverb of specification used with adjectives of derived verbs (II–X) and other derived words, such as abstract nouns with which the أفعل pattern rule, cannot be used. It requires little preparation and takes about 25 minutes to execute.

Procedure

1. Prepare a list of adjectives of derived verbs II–X and abstract nouns as many as there are students, with one adjective/noun on a separate index card/sheet of paper, and preferably add (in parentheses) the appropriate preposition to be used if needed and any other information next to the adjectives/nouns to further clarify their meanings so that comparisons can readily be made such as in the following list:

   مُدَرَّب (على السِّباحة)
   مُسافِر (إلى بلاد عربية)
   مُبْدِع (في الطبخ)
   مُتَكَلِّم
   مُتَسامِح (مع الفقراء)
   مُنْفَعِل (مع الأحْداث السياسية)
   مُحْتَرِم (للتَّقاليد)
   مُسْتَخْدِم (للأجهزة الإلكترونية)
   مَسْؤوليّة
   إنسانيّة

2. Divide your students into groups of 3 and distribute 3 cards to each group.
3. Ask members in each group to find out from each other and compare their own attributes with respect to the three adjectives/nouns that they received in the cards, with a total of nine sentences (in 9 minutes); for example, in the group that received the card with the adjective (مدرَّب على السباحة) "is trained/received training in swimming," one member is trained or not in swimming → مايكل مدرَّب أو غير مدرَّب على السباحة; another member is trained more than another جون أكثر تدرُّباً على السباحة من مايكل →; and a third member is trained the most أدم أكثر الطلاب في المجموعة/الأكثر تدرُّباً على السباحة.→

Grammar techniques   143

4. Ask each group to prepare/write three sets of three statements, using in each set of three statements one adjective/noun as an adverb of specification (used in the comparative and superlative about themselves).
5. If group members find the information in the parentheses too restrictive, they should ignore it and find some other attribute in common.
6. Go over your students' responses as a whole class, with each group member reporting to class a set of three statements pertaining to one adjective/noun comparing the three group members, with each group reporting a total of nine statements.
7. Elicit corrections from students of other groups.
8. Invite your students to ask questions about this structure and related ones.

Variations

a. Provide copies of the entire list to each student and ask each group to select three adjectives/nouns from the list.
b. Have a group exchange their statements with at least another group for corrections and comments.
c. Allow time for each group to incorporate the comments and corrections before each group reports their statements to the class.

25. *Identify the grammatical structures and vocalize them*
حدّدوا التراكيب وأعربوها

Purpose

To provide learners with deliberate practice in and review of a number of grammatical structures in context that they have learned recently or previously and their ability to recognize such structures as well as apply the relevant rules. The activity allows for the integration of deliberate grammar practice with the reading and possibly speaking skills. It requires little preparation and takes about 30 minutes to execute.

Procedure

1. Prepare a level-appropriate text or select one from your students' textbook or from Alhahawary (2016) containing a number of grammatical structures that they have learned recently and previously, such as those related to the number phrase, passive voice, quantifiers, the exceptive structure, the apposition structure, the exclamation structure, and the diptote, and mark all instances of the structure (e.g., by underlining, bolding, highlighting, or drawing a circle around them) as in the following text (excerpted from Taha Hussein's *The Days*):

كَانَ السِّيَاسِيُونَ أَعْضَاءِ الْوِزَارَةِ وَأَعْضَاءِ "الْوَفْدِ" يُؤْمِنُونَ جَمِيعاً بِحَقِّ مِصْرَ فِي الِاسْتِقْلَالِ، وَبِأَنَّ هَذَا الِاسْتِقْلَالَ يَجِبُ أَنْ يُسْتَخْلَصَ مِنَ الْإِنْجِلِيزِ بِالْمُفَاوَضَةِ الْحُرَّةِ إِيثَاراً لِلسِّلْمِ وَرَغْبَةً فِي الْعَافِيَةِ وَبُخْلاً بِالدِّمَاءِ عَلَى أَنْ تُرَاقَ وَبِالنُّفُوسِ عَلَى أَنْ تُزْهَقَ قَبْلَ أَنْ تُسْتَنْفَدَ وَسَائِلُ السِّلْمِ. وَلَكِنَّهُم عَلَى هَذَا الِاتِّفَاقِ وَالْإِجْمَاعِ كَانُوا يَخْتَلِفُونَ فِي مَظَاهِرِ هَذِهِ الْمُفَاوَضَةِ، لِأَنَّ مَنْ يُجْرِيها سَيُتَاحُ لَهُ تَحْقِيقِ الِاسْتِقْلَالِ إِنْ قُدِرَ لَهُ النَّجَاحِ.

وَكَذَلِكَ انْقَسَمَ الْمِصْرِيُّونَ وَثَارَتْ بَيْنَهُم فِتْنَةٌ مُنْكَرَةٌ جَعَلَتْ بَأْسَهُم بَيْنَهُم شَدِيدا. وَنَظَرَ صَاحِبُنا فَإِذَا الْعُلَمَاءُ وَالْمُفَكِّرُونَ كَغَيْرِهِم مِنَ النَّاسِ قَدِ انْقَسَمُوا إِلَى فَرِيقَيْنِ: فَرِيقٌ مِنْهُم مَالَ إِلَى الْوَفْدِ وَقَالَ مَعَ الْقَائِلِينَ: "لَا رَئِيسَ إِلَّا سَعْدٌ" وَفَرِيقٌ آخَرَ مَالَ إِلَى الْوِزَارَةِ وَقَالَ مَعَ الْقَائِلِينَ: "إِنَّمَا الْمُفَاوَضَاتُ لِمَنْ وُلِّيَ الْحُكْمِ". ثُمَّ نَظَرَ صَاحِبُنا فَإِذَا هُوَ كَغَيْرِهِ مِنْ عَامَةِ النَّاسِ، وَإِذَا هُوَ مَعَ الْفَرِيقِ الَّذِي مَالَ إِلَى الْوِزَارَةِ وَرَئِيسِها عَدْلِي بَاشَا، رَحِمَهُ اللهِ.

وَمَا أَسْرَعَ مَا اضْطَرَمَتِ الْفِتْنَةُ حَتَّى مَسَّ لَهْبُها كُلَّ نَفْسٍ وَكُلَّ عَقْلٍ وَكُلَّ ضَمِيرٍ. وَإِذَا الْوَفْدُ يَتَمَنَّى الْإِخْفَاقَ لِلْوِزَارَةِ فِي مُفَاوَضَاتِها وَيُدَبِّرُ لِهَذَا الْإِخْفَاقِ، وَإِذَا أَتْبَاعُ الْوَفْدِ يَجْهَرُونَ فِي غَيْرِ تَحَفُّظٍ بِدُعَائِهِم ذَاكَ الْبَغِيضِ: "الْحِمَايَةُ عَلَى يَدِ سَعْدٍ خَيْرٌ مِنَ الِاسْتِقْلَالِ عَلَى يَدِ عَدْلِي"! . . . .

وَيُنْفَى سَعْدٌ بَعْدَ إِخْفَاقِ عَدْلِي بِقَلِيلٍ، وَيُنْكِرُ عَدْلِي هَذَا الْإِخْفَاقَ، وَيُلِحُّ فِي قُبُولِ اسْتِقَالَتِهِ، وَيَرَى أَصْحَابُ عَدْلِي أَنَّ نَفْيَ سَعْدٍ إِهَانَةٌ لِلْوَطَنِ كُلِّهِ، وَتُوشِكُ الْكَلِمَةُ أَنْ تَجْتَمِعَ وَيُوشِكُ الْمِصْرِيُّونَ أَنْ يُصْبِحُوا يَداً وَاحِدَةً عَلَى خَصْمِهِم مِنَ الْإِنْجِلِيزِ. وَلَكِنَّ الْعَصَا لَا تَلْبَثُ أَنْ تَنْشَقَّ وَالْخِلَافَ لَا يَلْبَثُ أَنْ يَعُودَ كَأَعْنَفَ مَا كَانَ، لَمْ يُغَيِّرْ أَحَدُ الْفَرِيقَيْنِ مِنْ رَأْيِهِ وَلَا مِنْ خُطَّتِهِ شَيْئاً.

عَلَى أَنَّ تَصْرِيحَ الثَّامِنِ وَالْعِشْرِينَ مِنْ شَهْرِ فَبْرَايِرَ سَنَةَ اثْنَتَيْنِ وَعِشْرِينَ وَتِسْعِ مِئَةٍ وَأَلْفٍ يَرُدُّ إِلَى الْعَدْلِيِّينَ شَيْئاً مِنْ ثِقَةٍ وَكَثِيراً مِنْ أَمَلٍ. فَقَدْ ظَفِرَ ثَرْوَت بَاشَا- رَحِمَهُ اللهُ- بِبَعْضِ الْحَقِّ. وَشَيْءٌ خَيْرٌ مِنْ لَا شَيْءٍ! . . . .

وَالْخِلَافُ يَمْضِي فِي طَرِيقِهِ لَا تَهْدَأُ ثَوْرَتُهُ وَلَا تَزْدَادُ نَارُهُ إِلَّا اضْطِرَامٍ، وَصَاحِبُنا مَاضٍ مَعَ أَصْحَابِهِ فِي إِذْكَاءِ هَذِهِ النَّارِ لَا يَعْنِيهِ أَنْ يَرْضَى عَنْهُ الرَّاضُونَ أَوْ يَسْخَطَ عَلَيْهِ السَّاخِطُونَ، وَإِنَّمَا هُوَ مُقْتَنِعٌ بِأَنَّ شَيْئاً خَيْرٌ مِنْ لَا شَيْءٍ، وَبِأَنَّ الْقَلِيلَ صَائِرٌ إِلَى الْكَثِيرِ، وَبِأَنَّ هَذِهِ الْمَظَاهِرَ سَتُصْبِحُ فِي يَوْمٍ مِنَ الْأَيَّامِ حَقَائِقَ إِنْ عَرَفَ الْمِصْرِيُّونَ كَيْفَ يَحْزِمُونَ أُمُورَهُم وَكَيْفَ يُجْمِعُونَ كَلِمَتَهُم وَكَيْفَ يُحْسِنُونَ انْتِهَازَ الْفُرَصِ.

2. Provide copies of the text and display it on the screen or via a document projector.
3. Divide your students into dyads and have half the groups (Group A) discuss and name the structures of the underlined words and the other half (Group B) supply their case endings (in about 10 minutes).
4. Redivide the groups into new dyads so that each new group consists of a student from Group A paired with a student from Group B and ask them to discuss and finalize their answers (in about 10 minutes).

Grammar techniques   145

5. Go over your students' responses as a whole class by having each group delegate a student to read a sentence, vocalize the underlined word(s) fully, and name the grammatical structure(s) contained in the sentence.
6. Elicit corrections from students of other groups.
7. Invite questions from your students about the targeted structures and similar ones.

Variations

a. Instead of providing all instances of the target structures marked in the text, remove all such markings and ask your students to identify a given number of instances of the structures, such as identifying four instances of the number phrase, four of the passive voice, two quantifiers, two of the exceptive structure, three of the apposition structure, one of the exclamation structure, and two of the diptote, and vocalize them correctly.
b. Have your students only name a subset of the structures contained in the text, provide the text without vowels, and ask your students to vocalize a portion of the text that contains structures that are the target of this activity/text.

(See Alhawary 2016.)

Appendix A

Correction symbols: intermediate level

رموز ملاحظات التصحيح للمتعلِّمين في المستوى المتوسِّط

خطأ في الإضافة	إض
خطأ في الإعراب	إع
خطأ في التعريف أو التنكير	ت
خطأ في ترتيب الكلمات	تر
حذف الكلمة أو الكلمات	ح
خطأ في الدلالة/اختيار الكلمة	د
خطأ لعدم وجود أداة ربط	ر
خطأ في زمن الفعل	ز
خطأ في ضمير عائد	ع
استخدام للعامية	عم
خطأ في الكتابة	ك
خطأ في المطابقة	م
خطأ في الاسم الموصول/جملة اسم الموصول	مو
سهو عن كلمة أو عبارة	ـه
خطأ في الوزن (وزن الاسم أو الصفة أو الفعل)	و

Appendix B

Correction symbols:
advanced level

رموز ملاحظات التصحيح للمتعلِّمين في
المستوى المتقدِّم

خطأ في الإضافة	إض
خطأ في الإعراب	إع
خطأ في التعريف أو التنكير	ت
تداخل في التراكيب	تد
خطأ في ترتيب الكلمات	تر
حذف الكلمة أو الكلمات	ح
خطأ في الدلالة/اختيار الكلمة	د
خطأ لعدم وجود أداة ربط	ر
خطأ في زمن الفعل	ز
خطأ في ظرف الزمان أو المكان	ظ
خطأ في ضمير عائد	ع
خطأ في العدد أو المعدود	عد
استخدام العامية	عم
فقرة جديدة	ف
خطأ في الكتابة	ك
خطأ في المطابقة	م
المعنى مبهم	مب
خطأ في الاسم الموصول/جملة اسم الموصول	مو
سهو عن كلمة أو عبارة	ـه
خطأ في الوزن (وزن الاسم أو الصفة أو الفعل)	و

Bibliography and resources for further reading

ACTFL (American Council on the Teaching of Foreign Languages). 2012. *ACTFL Proficiency Guidelines.* [www.actfl.org/resources/actfl-proficiency-guidelines-2012/arabic].
Akil II, Bakari R. 2010. *Speech Exercises for the Classroom: A Guide for Professors, Teachers and Speech Instructors.* N.P.: Academic Group Publishing.
Alfieri, Louis, Brooks, Patricia J., Aldrich, Naomi J., and Tenenbaum, Harriet. 2011. "Does Discovery Based Instruction Enhance Learning?". *Journal of Educational Psychology* 103 (1): 1–18.
Alhawary, Mohammad T. 2011. *Modern Standard Arabic Grammar: A Learner's Guide.* West Sussex, UK: Wiley-Blackwell.
Alhawary, Mohammad T. 2013. "Arabic Second Language Acquisition Research and Second Language Teaching: What the Teacher, Textbook Writer, and Tester Need to Know". *Al-'Arabiyya* 46: 23–35.
Alhawary, Mohammad T. 2016. *Arabic Grammar in Context.* Oxon, UK: Routledge.
Al-Sheikh, Hanan. 2005. *My Story Is a Lon Explanation* [ḥikāyatī sharḥun yaṭūl]. Beirut, Lebanon: Dār Al-Ādāb.
Anderson, Neil J. 2009. "Active Reading: The Research Base for a Pedagogical Approach in the Reading Classroom". In Zhaohong Han and Neil J. Anderson, eds., *Second Language Reading Research and Instruction: Crossing the Boundaries.* Ann Arbor, MI: The University of Michigan Press.
Anderson, Neil J. 2012. "Reading Instruction". In Anne Burns and Jack C. Richards, eds., *The Cambridge Guide to Pedagogy and Practice in Second Language Acquisition*, 218–225. Cambridge, UK: Cambridge University Press.
Aronson, Elliot. 1978. *The Jigsaw Classroom.* Beverly Hills, CA: Sage.
Atay, Derin and Kurt, Gokce. 2006. "Elementary School EFL Learners' Vocabulary Learning: The Effects of Post-Reading Activities". *Canadian Modern Language Review* 63 (2): 255–273.
Bahram, Zaitoon. 2020. "Classroom Techniques and Tasks for Teaching Speaking". *International Journal of Science and Research* 9 (1): 432–434.
Bello, Tom. 1997. *Improving ESL Learners' Writing Skills.* Washington, DC: National Clearinghouse for ESL Literacy Education.
Berne, Jane E. 1998. "Examining the Relationship between L2 Listening Research, Pedagogical Theory and Practice". *Foreign Language Annals* 32: 169–190.
Berne, Jane E. 2004. "Listening Comprehension Strategies: A Review of the Literature". *Foreign Language Annals* 37 (4): 521–531.
Bilbrough, Nick. 2007. *Dialogue Activities: Exploring Spoken Interaction in the Language Class.* Cambridge, UK: Cambridge University Press.

Bibliography and resources for further reading 149

Blanchard, Karen and Root, Christine. 2010. *Ready to Write 2: Perfecting Paragraphs*. White Plains, NY: Pearson Education.

Blaz, Deborah. 2018. *The World Language Teacher's Guide to Active Learning: Strategies and Activities for Increasing Student Engagement*. Oxon, UK: Routledge.

Blundell, Lesley and Stokes, Jackie. 1981. *Task Listening*. Cambridge, UK: Cambridge University Press.

Bode, Gary, Whitley, Charles G., and James, Gary. 1981. *Listening in & Speaking Out*. Essex, UK: Longman.

Bolen, Jackie. 2015. *39 No-Prep/Low-Prep ESL Speaking Activities: For Teenagers and Adults*. N.P.: Jackie Bolen.

British Council. 2015. "A Few Discussion Activities for English Language Learners". www.britishcouncil.org/voices-magazine/few-discussion-activities-english-language-Learners.

Brookes, Arthur and Grundy, Peter. 1998. *Beginning to Write: Writing Activities for Elementary and Intermediate Learners*. Cambridge, UK: Cambridge University Press.

Brown, Gillian. 1986. "Investigating Listening Comprehension in Context". *Applied Linguistics* 7 (3): 284–302.

Brown, H. Douglas. 2001. *Teaching by Principles: An Interactive Approach to Language Pedagogy*. White Plains, NY: Longman.

Bygate, Martin. 1987. *Speaking (Language Teaching: A Scheme for Teaching Education)*. Oxford, UK: Oxford University Press.

Bygate, Martin. 2010. "Speaking." In Robert B. Kaplan, ed., *The Oxford Handbook of Applied Linguistics*, 63–74. Oxford, UK: Oxford University Press.

Byrne, Donn. 1978. *Listening Comprehension Practice*. Essex, UK: Longman.

Celce-Murcia, Marianne and Hilles, Sharon. 1988. *Techniques and Resources in Teaching Grammar*. Oxford: Oxford University Press.

Chambers, Fred and Brigham, Andrew. 1989. "Summary Writing: A Short Cut to Success". *English Teaching Forum* 27 (1): 43–45.

Clark, Raymond C. 1980. *Language Teaching Techniques*. Vermont: Pro Lingua.

Cobb, David, Methold, Chuntana, and Methold, Kenneth. 1979. *Puzzles for English Practice*. London, UK: Longman.

Coleman, James A. and Klapper, John. 2004. *Effective Learning and Teaching in Modern Languages*. Oxon, UK: Routledge.

Correia, Rosane. 2006. "Encouraging Critical Reading in the EFL Classroom". *English Teaching Forum* 44 (1): 16–19.

Cumming, Alister, Rebuffot, Jacques, and Monica Ledwell. 1989. "Reading and Summarizing Challenging Texts in First and Second Languages". *Reading and Writing* 1: 201–219.

Curfs, Emile. 1982. "Listening Deserves Better". *Modern English Teacher* 9 (3): 11–14.

Davis, Paul and Rinvolucri, Mario. 1988. *Dictation: New Methods, New Possibilities*. Cambridge, UK: Cambridge University Press.

Day, Richard R. and Park Jeong-suk. 2005. "Developing Reading Comprehension Questions". *Reading in a Foreign Language* 17 (1): 60–73.

Díaz-Rico, Lynne T. 2013. *Strategies for Teaching English Learners*. Boston, MA: Pearson.

Doff, Adrian and Becket, Carolyn. 1991. *Cambridge Skills for Fluency: Listening*. Cambridge, UK: Cambridge University Press.

Elkhafaifi, Hussein. 2005a. "The Effects of Prelistening Activities on Listening Comprehension in Arabic Learners". *Foreign Language Annals* 38 (4): 505–513.

Elkhafaifi, Hussein. 2005b. "Listening Comprehension and Anxiety in the Arabic Language Classroom". *The Modern Language Journal* 89 (2): 206–220.

150 Bibliography and resources for further reading

Elkhafaifi, Hussein. 2007–8. "An Exploration of Listening Strategies: A Descriptive Study of Arabic Learners". *Al-'Arabiyya* 40–41: 71–86.

El-Koumy, Abdel Salam. 1999. "Effects of Three Semantic Mapping Strategies on EFL Students Reading Comprehension". *Education Resource Information Center*. http://ssrn.com/abstract=2365006

Ellis, Rod. 1991. *Second Language Acquisition & Language Pedagogy*. Clevedon, UK: Multilingual Matters.

Emmerson, Paul and Hamilton, Nick. 2005. *Five-Minute Activities for Business English*. Cambridge, UK: Cambridge University Press.

Epstein, Ruth. 1991. *Literacy through Cooperative Learning: The Jigsaw Reading Technique*. Saskatoon, SK, Canada: Center for School-Based Programs, College of Education, University of Saskatchewan.

Etsuo, Taguchi, Gorsuch, Greta, Lems, Kristin, and Rory Rosszell, R. 2016. "Scaffolding in L2 Reading: How Repetition and an Auditory Model Help Readers". *Reading in a Foreign Language* 28 (1): 101–117.

Faber, Sharon H. 2015. *How to Teach Reading When You're Not a Reading Teacher*. Nashville, TN: World Book.

Field, John. 1998. "Skills and Strategies: Towards a New Methodology for Listening". *English Language Teaching Journal* 54 (2): 110–118.

Field, John. 2004. "An Insight into Listeners' Problems: Too Much Bottom-Up or Too Much Top-Down". *System* 36: 35–51.

Field, John. 2008. *Listening in the Language Classroom*. Cambridge, UK: Cambridge University Press.

Fisher, Douglas, Frey, Nancy, and Diane Lapp. 2011. *Teaching Students to Read Like Detectives: Comprehending, Analyzing, and Discussing Text*. Bloomington, IN: Solution Tree.

Flenley, Tony. 1982. "Making Realistic Listening Material". *Modern English Teacher* 10 (2): 14–15.

Fotos, Sandra S. 1994. "Integrating Grammar Instruction and Communicative Language Use through Grammar Consciousness-Raising Tasks". *TESOL Quarterly* 28 (2): 323–351.

Gairns, Ruth and Redman, Stuart. 1986. *Working with Words: A Guide to Teaching and Learning Vocabulary*. Cambridge, UK: Cambridge University Press.

Geddes, Marion and Sturtridge, Gill. 1979. *Listening Links*. London, UK: Heinemann.

Ghasemi, Parvin. 2011. "Teaching the Short Story to Improve L2 Reading and Writing Skills: Approaches and Strategies". *International Journal of Arts and Sciences* 4 (18): 265–273.

Goh, Christine. 2008. "Metacognitive Instruction for Second Language Listening Development: Theory, Practice and Research Implications". *RELC Journal* 39 (2): 188–213.

Goh, Christine and Yusnita, Taib. 2006. "Metacognitive Instruction in Listening for Young Learners". *English Language Teaching Journal* 60 (3): 222–232.

Gorsuch, Greta, Taguchi, Etsuo, and Umehara, Hiroaki. 2015. "Repeated Reading for Japanese Language Learners: Effects on Reading Speed, Comprehension, and Comprehension strategies". *The Reading Matrix* 15 (2): 18–44.

Grabe, William. 2004. "Research on Teaching Reading". *Annual Review of Applied Linguistics* 24: 44–69.

Grabe, William. 2009. *Reading in a Second Language: Moving from Theory to Practice*. Cambridge, UK: Cambridge University Press.

Green, Peter S. and Hecht, Karlheinz. 1992. "Implicit and Explicit Grammar: An Empirical Study". *Applied Linguistics* 13 (2): 168–184.

Bibliography and resources for further reading   151

Hadfield, Jill. 1984. *Elementary Communication Games*. Essex, UK: Pearson.

Hammadou, Joann. 2000. "The Impact of Analogy and Content Knowledge on Reading Comprehension: What Helps, What Hurts". *The Modern Language Journal* 84 (1): 38–50.

Hammerly, Hector. 1985. *An Integrated Theory of Language Teaching and Its Practical Consequences*. Blaine, WA: Second Language Publications.

Harmer, Jeremy. 2004. *How to Teach Writing*. Essex, UK: Pearson Education.

Hewitt, Ian E. 1996. *Edutainment: How to Teach Language with Fun and Games*. Subiaco WA, Australia: Language Direct.

Hillerich, Robert L. 1988. *Elementary Teacher's Language Arts Handbook: Techniques and Ideas for Teaching: Teaching Reading as a Language Art*. Englewood Cliffs, NJ: Prentice Hall.

Hinkel, Eli. 2010. "Integrating the Four Skills: Current and Historical Perspectives". In Robert B. Kaplan, ed., *The Oxford Handbook of Applied Linguistics*, 110–126. Oxford, UK: Oxford University Press.

Hodges, Gabrielle C. 2016. "Becoming Poetry Teachers: Studying Poems through Choral Reading". *Changing English* 23 (4): 375–386.

Huang, Ching-Ting and Yang, Shu Ching. 2015. "Effects of Online Reciprocal Teaching on Reading Strategies, Comprehension, Self-Efficacy, and Motivation". *Journal of Educational Computing Research* 52 (3): 381–407.

Hussein, Taha. n.d. *The Days* ['al-'ayyam]. Cairo: Egypt: Dār Al-Ma'ārif.

Jenkins, Jennifer. 2004. "Research in Teaching Pronunciation and Intonation". *Annual Review of Applied Linguistics* 24: 109–125.

József, Horváth. 2001. *Advanced Writing in English as a Foreign Language: A Corpus-Based Study of Processes and Products*. Pécs, Hungary: Lingua Franca Csoport.

Kayi, Hayriye. 2006. "Teaching Speaking: Activities to Promote Speaking in a Second Language". *The Internet TESL Journal* 12 (11): 1–6.

Klippel, Friederike. 1984. *Keep Talking: Communicative Fluency Activities for Language Teaching*. Cambridge, UK: Cambridge University Press.

Krashen, Stephen and Terrell, Tracy D. 1983. *The Natural Approach: Language Acquisition in the Classroom*. Oxford, UK: Pergamon.

Labmeier, Angela M. and Vockell, Edward L. 1971. *Effects and Correlates of a Course in Speed Reading*. West Lafayette, IA: Purdue University.

Larsen-Freeman, Diane. 2003. *Teaching Language: From Grammar to Grammaring*. Boston, MA: Heinle.

Larsen-Freeman, Diane. 2011. *Techniques and Principles in Language Teaching: Teaching Techniques in English as a Second Language*. Oxford, UK: Oxford University Press.

Leki, Ilona. 2010. "Second Language Writing in English". In Robert B. Kaplan, ed., *The Oxford Handbook of Applied Linguistics*, 100–110. Oxford, UK: Oxford University Press.

Lindstromberg, Seth. 2009. *Language Activities for Teenagers*. Cambridge, UK: Cambridge University Press.

Liu, Yeu-Ting and Todd, Andrew Graeme. 2014. "Implementation of Assisted Repeated Reading Techniques for the Incidental Acquisition of Novel Foreign Vocabulary". *Language Teaching Research* 20 (1): 53–74.

Long, Michael H. 1988. "Instructed Interlanguage Development". In Leslie M. Beebe, ed., *Issues in Second Language Acquisition: Multiple Perspectives*, 115–141. Rowley: Newbury House.

Lund, Randall J. 1990. "A Taxonomy for Teaching Second Language Listening". *Foreign Language Annals* 23: 105–115.

152 Bibliography and resources for further reading

Lynch, Tony. 1983. *Study Listening*. Cambridge, UK: Cambridge University Press.

Lynch, Tony. 2010. "Listening: Sources, Skills, and Strategies". In Robert B. Kaplan, ed., *The Oxford Handbook of Applied Linguistics*, 74–87. Oxford, UK: Oxford University Press.

Macalister, John. 2010. "Speed Reading Courses and Their Effect on Reading Authentic Texts: A Preliminary Investigation". *Reading in a Foreign Language* 22 (1): 104–116.

Maley, Alan. 1978. "The Teaching of Listening Comprehension Skills". *Modern English Teacher* 6 (3): 6–9.

Maley, Alan and Duff, Alan. 1979. *Variations on a Theme*. Cambridge, UK: Cambridge University Press.

Maley, Alan and Duff, Alan. 2010. *Drama Techniques: A Resource Book of Communication Activities for Language Teachers*. Cambridge, UK: Cambridge University Press.

Maley, Alan and Moulding, Sandra. 1981. *Learning to Listen*. Cambridge, UK: Cambridge University Press.

Manoli, Polyxeni and Papadopoulou, Maria. 2012. "Graphic Organizers as a Reading Strategy: Research Findings and Issues". *Creative Education* 3 (3): 348–356.

McCarthy, Michael and O'Keefe, Anne. 2004. "Research in the Teaching of Speaking". *Annual Review of Applied Linguistics* 24: 26–43.

McDonough, Jo and Shaw, Christopher. 1993. *Materials and Methods in ELT: A Teacher's Guide*. Oxford, UK: Blackwell.

McKay, Penny and Guse, Jenni. 2007. *Five-Minute Activities for Young Learners*. Cambridge, UK: Cambridge University Press.

Mendelsohn, David J. and Rubin, Joan. 1995. *A Guide for the Teaching of Second Language Listening*. Carlsbad, CA: Dominie Press.

Morley, Joan. 1984. *Listening and Language Learning in ESL: Developing Self-Study Activities for Listening Comprehension*. Orlando, FL: Harcourt Brace Jovanovich.

Morley, Joan. 1991. "Language Skills: A. Listening". In Marianne Celcia-Murcia, ed., *Teaching English as a Second or Foreign Language*, 81–106. Boston, MA: Newbury.

Mortimer, Colin. 1984. *Elements of Pronunciation*. Cambridge, UK: Cambridge University Press.

Moskowitz, Gertrude. 1978. *Sharing and Caring in the Foreign Language Class: A Sourcebook on Humanistic Techniques*. Rowley, MA: Newbury House.

Nassaji, Hossein and Fotos, Sandra S. 2004. "Current Developments in Research on the Teaching of Grammar". *Annual Review of Applied Linguistics* 24: 126–145.

Nassaji, Hossein and Fotos, Sandra S. 2011. *Teaching Grammar in Second Language Classrooms: Integrating Form-Focused Instruction in Communicative Context*. Oxon, UK: Routledge.

Nation, Ian Stephen Paul. 1978. "'What Is It?' A Multipurpose Language Teaching Technique". *English Teaching Forum* 16 (3): 20–23, 32.

Nation, Ian Stephen Paul. 1985. "Listening Techniques for a Comprehension Approach to Language Learning". *English Teaching Forum* 23 (4): 17–21.

Nation, Ian Stephen Paul. 2009. *Teaching ESL/EFL Reading and Writing*. Oxon, UK: Routledge.

Nation, Ian Stephen Paul and Newton, Jonathan M. 2020. *Teaching ESL/EFL Listening and Speaking*. Oxon, UK: Routledge.

Norris, William E. 1970. "Teaching Second Language Reading at the Advanced Level: Goals, Techniques and Procedures". *TESOL Quarterly* 4 (1): 17–35.

Nuttall, Christine. 2005. *Teaching Reading Skills in a Foreign Language*. Oxford, UK: Macmillan.

Bibliography and resources for further reading   153

Ockenden, Michael. 1977. *Talking Points*. Essex, UK: Longman.

Ogle, Donna. 1986. "K-W-L: A Teaching Model That Develops Active Reading of Expository Text". *The Reading Teacher* 39 (6): 564–570.

Omaggio Hadley, Alice. 2001. *Teaching Language in Context*. Boston, MA: Heinle & Heinle.

Oshima, Alice and Hogue, Ann. 2006. *Writing Academic English*. White Plains, NY: Pearson Longman.

Palincsar, Annemarie Sullivan and Brown, Ann L. 1986. "Interactive Teaching to Promote Independent Learning from Text". *Reading Teacher* 20 (1): 771–776.

Papalia, Anthony. 1987. "Interaction of Reader and Text". In Wilga M. Rivers, ed., *Interactive Language Teaching*, 70–82. Cambridge, UK: Cambridge University Press.

Pearson, P. David and Johnson, Dale D. 1978. *Teaching Reading Comprehension*. New York: Holt, Rinehart, and Winston.

Porter, Don and Roberts, Jon. 1981. "Authentic Listening Activities". *English Language Teaching Journal* 36 (1): 37–47.

Prabhu, N. S. 1987. *Second Language Pedagogy*. Oxford, UK: Oxford University Press.

Prator, Clifford H. 1974. "In Search of a Method". *Workpapers in Teaching English as a Second Language* 9: 13–25.

Qasim, Abdulhakim. 1984. *The Guided One* [al-mahdī]. Beirut, Lebanon: Dār Al-Tanwīr Li-Al-Ṭibāʿa wa Al-Nashr.

Ramage, Gill. 2012. *The Modern Languages Teacher's Handbook*. London, UK: Continuum.

Rammuny, Raji. 1985. "Successful Teaching Strategies for Developing the Speaking Skills in the Teaching of Modern Standard Arabic". *Al-ʿArabiyya* 18 (1/2): 29–68.

Raymond, C. Clark. 1987. *Language Teaching Techniques*. Brattleboro, VT: Pro Lingua.

Reichenberg, Monica. 2008. "Making Students Talk about Expository Texts". *Scandinavian Journal of Educational Research* 52 (1): 17–39.

Richards, Jack C. 1983. "Listening Comprehension: Approach, Design, Procedure". *TESOL Quarterly* 17: 219–239.

Ridgway, Tony. 2000. "Listening Strategies: I Beg Your Pardon?". *English Language Teaching Journal* 54 (2): 179–185.

Riechelt, Melinda. 1999. "Toward a More Comprehensive View of L2 Writing: Foreign Language Writing in the U.S.". *Journal of Second Language Writing* 8 (2): 181–204.

Rivers, Wilga M. 1987. *Interactive Language Teaching*. Cambridge, UK: Cambridge University Press.

Rosenshine, Barak, Meister, Carla, and Chapman, Saul. 1996. "Teaching Students to Generate Questions: A Review of the Intervention Studies". *Review of Educational Research* 66 (2): 181–221.

Russo, Gloria M. 1987. "Writing: An Interactive Experience". In Wilga M. Rivers, ed., *Interactive Language Teaching*, 83–92. Cambridge, UK: Cambridge University Press.

Rusterholz, Barbara L. 1987. "Reading Strategies for Business Foreign Language Class". *Foreign Language Annals* 20 (5): 427–433.

Ryding, Karin C. 2013. *Teaching and Learning Arabic as a Foreign Language: A Guide for Teachers*. Washington, DC: Georgetown University Press.

Seliger, Herbert W. 1983. "Learner Interaction in the Classroom and Its Effects on Language Acquisition". In Herbert W. Seliger and Michael H. Long, eds., *Classroom Oriented Research in Second Language Acquisition*, 246–267. Rowley, MA: Newbury House.

Seng, Goh Hock. 2007. "The Effects of Think-Aloud in a Collaborative Environment to Improve Comprehension of L2 Texts". *The Reading Matrix* 7 (2): 29–54.

154 Bibliography and resources for further reading

Sepulveda, Janine. 2012. *Fifty Ways to Teach Listening: Tips for ESL/EFL Teachers*. Katoomba, NSW, Australia: Wayzgoose Press.

Seymour, David and Popova, Maria. 2005. *700 Classroom Activities: Instant Lessons for Busy Teachers*. Oxford, UK: Macmillan.

Sheerin, Susan. 1987. "Listening Comprehension: Teaching or Testing?". *English Language Teaching Journal* 41 (2): 126–131.

Shiang, Ruei-Fang. 2018. "Embodied EFL Reading Activity: Let's Produce Comics". *Reading in a Foreign Language* 30 (1): 108–129.

Silberstein, Sandra. 1994. *Techniques and Resources in Teaching Reading*. New York, NY: Oxford University Press.

Silva, Tony and Brice, Colleen. 2004. "Research in Teaching Writing". *Annual Review of Applied Linguistics* 24: 70–106.

Stokes, Jacqueline St. Clair. 1984. *Elementary Task Listening*. Cambridge, UK: Cambridge University Press.

Syakur, Abd. 2020. "Improving the Eighth Grade Students' Listening Comprehension Achievement by Using Dictation Techniques". *Konfrontasi: Jurnal Kultural, Ekonomi dan Perubahan Sosial* 7 (3): 205–216.

Szabo, Susan. 2006. "KWHHL: A Student-Driven Evolution of the KWL". *American Secondary Education* 34 (3): 57–66.

Thornbury, Scott. 1999. *How to Teach Grammar*. Essex, UK: Pearson Education.

Thornbury, Scott. 2005. *How to Teach Speaking*. Essex, UK: Pearson Education.

Tsou, Wenli. 2005. "Improving Speaking Skills through Instruction in Oral Classroom Participation". *Foreign Language Annals* 38 (1): 46–55.

Underwood, Mary and Barr, Pauline. 1980. *Listeners*. Oxford, UK: Oxford University Press.

Upton, Thomas A. 2004. *Reading Skills for Success: A Guide to Academic Texts*. Ann Arbor, MI: University of Michigan Press.

Ur, Penny. 1984. *Teaching Listening Comprehension*. Cambridge, UK: Cambridge University Press.

Ur, Penny. 2007. *Discussions That Work: Task-Centered Fluency Practice*. Cambridge, UK: Cambridge University Press.

Ur, Penny. 2009. *Grammar Practice Activities Paperback with CD-ROM: A Practical Guide for Teachers*. Cambridge, UK: Cambridge University Press.

Ur, Penny and Wright, Andrew. 1992. *Five-Minute Activities: A Resource Book of Short Activities*. Cambridge, UK: Cambridge University Press.

Urquhart, Vicki and Frazee, Dana. 2012. *Teaching Reading in the Content Areas: If Not Me, Then Who?* Alexandria, VA: ASCD.

Vandergrift, Larry. 2002. "'It Was Nice to See That Our Predictions Were Right': Developing Metacognition in L2 Listening Comprehension". *Canadian Modern Language Review* 58: 555–575.

Vandergrift, Larry. 2004. "Listening to Learn or Learning to Listen?". *Annual Review of Applied Linguistics* 24: 3–25.

Vandergrift, Laurens. 1997. "The Cinderella of Communicative Strategies: Reception Strategies in Interactive Listening". *The Modern Language Journal* 81 (4): 494–505.

Vásquez, Anete, Hansen, Angela L., and Smith, Philip C. 2010. *Teaching Language Arts to English Language Learners*. Oxon, UK: Routledge.

Vernon, Shelley Ann. 2012. *ESL Classroom Activities for Teens & Adults: Fluency Activities and Grammar Drills for EFL and ESL Students*. N.P.: Shelley S. Vernon.

Bibliography and resources for further reading   155

Watkins, Peter. 2018. *Teaching and Developing Reading Skills*. Cambridge, UK: Cambridge University Press.

Weaver, Constance. 1996. *Teaching Grammar in Context*. Portsmouth, NH: Boynton/Cook.

Weissberg, Robert. 2006. *Connecting Speaking & Writing in Second Language Writing Instruction*. Ann Arbor, MI: University of Michigan Press.

Wilson, J. J. 2008. *How to Teach Listening*. Essex, UK: Longman.

Woodward, Suzanne W. 1997. *Fun with Grammar: Communicative Activities for the Azar Grammar Series*. Upper Saddle River, NJ: Prentice Hall Regents.

Woytak, Lidia. 1984. "Reading Proficiency and Psycholinguistic Approach to Second Language Reading". *Foreign Language Annals* 17 (5): 509–517.

Wright, Andrew. 1989. *Pictures for Language Learning*. Cambridge, UK: Cambridge University Press.

Wright, Andrew, Betteridge, David, and Buckby, Michael. 2006. *Games for Language Learning*. Cambridge, UK: Cambridge University Press.

Yang, Yingjie. 2014. "The Development of Speaking Fluency: The 4/3/2 Technique for the EFL Learners in China". *International Journal of Research Studies in Language Learning* 3 (4): 55–70.

Yildirim, Sefa and Soylemez, Yusuf. 2018. "The Effect of Performing Reading Activities with Critical Reading Questions on Critical Thinking and Reading Skills". *Asian Journal of Education and Training* 4 (4): 326–335.

Index

accuracy 29, 33, 45, 56, 65, 78–79, 84, 86, 107–108
ACTFL guidelines 1, 33, 60, 84
adjectives 47, 124, 128, 142–143; *see also* noun-adjective phrase
advanced organizers 4, 17, 27, 30–31; *see also* listening, pre-listening
advantages and disadvantages 56–58, 83, 109–110
adverbs: manner 135, 142–143; place 115, 127; specification 134; time 99, 112, 115, 127
anxiety 26, 37, 48, 49, 52
apposition structure 138, 143, 145
Arabic: colloquial varieties 2; Modern Standard Arabic 2

background: experience 81–82, 105–106; knowledge 60, 81–82; noise 21–22
boredom 4, 111, 125, 137
brainstorming 30, 106–107, 109–110

case endings 66, 113–115, 118, 123, 130–131, 134, 136, 138, 144
classroom equipment: document projector 13–14, 23, 28, 38–40, 44–45, 53, 61–62, 69, 71–72, 78, 85–86, 88–89, 97–98, 101–104, 113–114, 116–117, 122, 125, 129, 132, 134, 136, 138–140, 144; screen 5, 10, 13, 28, 38–39, 45, 61–62, 71–72, 85–86, 88, 104, 113–114, 116, 120, 125, 132, 134, 139, 144; slides 44, 112, 116, 139
classroom management 2
clauses (embedded) 131–132
commands 18–19; *see also* imperative; negative imperative

communicative: functional ability 33, 35–36, 38–41, 111, 124, 137; functional needs 33, 84
communicative approach 1, 111, 124, 137
comparative and superlative degrees 127, 142–143
comparing 24, 28, 49, 79, 80, 89, 107–109, 128, 142–143
complexity 11, 33, 84
conditional sentences 49, 135–136, 138–140
conjunctions 13, 51, 106
connectors 51, 55, 96–97, 99, 101–102, 106–107, 133
consonants: emphatic 5–6, 9–10, 14; nonemphatic 5–6, 9–10, 14; *see also* phonemic contrasts
context 2, 6, 30–32, 49, 60, 62, 116, 118, 133, 143
contrasting 107–109
copying 14, 85, 87, 110, 124, 137

debating 32, 58, 59
definiteness: definite 12, 21, 114, 118–119, 132, 135; indefinite 12, 121, 134–136; moon letters 12; sun letters 12
deliberate practice 111, 113–116, 118, 120–127, 129–133, 135–140, 142–143
describing 15, 19, 37–38, 41, 48, 57, 82
diacritics (internal short vowels) 63, 85, 145
dialogues 22–23, 29–30, 36, 46–47, 63, 98–99
dictation 13–14, 20, 23–24, 26–28, 88–90
diptote 138, 143, 145
discourse 23, 119; extended discourse, level 27, 33, 54, 56–58, 78, 84, 105, 108–109; production 84, 105

Index   157

English: language 36, 42, 44, 61, 121, 135; speakers 10
error correction 38, 40, 45, 47, 53–54, 86, 112, 123–124, 132, 136–137, 139–1
errors 21, 38, 40, 45, 47, 53–54, 58, 65, 86, 88, 102–103, 106–107, 123–124, 127, 132, 136–137, 140–141
exceptive structure 138, 143, 145
exclamation structure 138, 143, 145
expository texts 78–79
expressing 35, 38–39, 82, 94, 99, 109, 127, 142

feedback 12–13, 16–17, 19, 22–23, 28–29, 38–40, 45–46, 47–49, 51–52, 55, 57–58, 73, 78–80, 83, 87, 93, 95, 98–100, 103–110
fluency 28–41, 33, 35–36, 44, 46, 48–49, 51–53, 56–57, 60, 63–64, 66, 68, 73, 84, 86, 88–91, 94–95, 97–109, 140
form 2, 15, 27, 31–32, 54, 78, 105, 107, 111–112, 116, 121, 125–131, 136
function 2, 27, 31–32, 54, 59, 78, 94, 105, 109, 111

games 19, 61
gisting 25, 28, 78–79, 98
grammar 2, 33, 38, 42, 66, 73, 76, 84, 111–145
grammatical agreement 82, 113, 120, 124, 136
greetings 17, 33–35, 62
guessing 19–21, 31–32, 40, 47, 67, 72, 116–118

'idāfa 114–115, 118–119, 121, 123, 129, 135
imperative 125–126
'inna and its sisters 130–131
introductions 33–35

kāna and its sisters 130–131

listening: during-listening 4, 17, 27; post-listening 4, 17, 27, 31–32; pre-listening 4, 17, 27, 30–31

memorized chunks: level 4, 33, 60, 63, 84; production 33, 64, 84; recognition 4, 60
mimicking 28, 35, 78–79, 100
minimal pairs 7, 9–10, 14

modeling 34, 38, 86–87, 112, 115, 122, 125, 136, 139
mood endings 66, 118, 124, 131, 134, 136, 138

narrating 24–25
narrative texts 47, 51, 78–79, 98–99
negation: future 126–127; past tense 99, 126–127; present tense 99, 126–127; verbless sentence 127
negative imperative 125–126
noun-adjective phrase 113, 118, 121, 123
noun phrase 123, 132; see also apposition structure; 'idāfa; noun-adjective phrase
nouns: abstract 142; defective 136; five nouns 136; subject 96; unique 119; verbal 129–130
number phrase 135–136, 138, 143, 145

paragraph: level 4, 17, 27, 33, 44, 54–55, 84, 95, 97–99, 101–102, 105; production 33, 44, 54, 84, 95, 105; recognition 4, 23
paraphrasing 103–104
pattern wazn 116, 117–118, 125, 127, 142
personalizing 41–42
phonemic contrasts 9–10
phrase: level 4, 60, 63, 84–86, 111, 125; production 33, 84; recognition 4, 17, 20, 27, 60; see also apposition structure; 'idāfa; noun phrase; noun-adjective phrase
prepositions 13, 88, 112, 115, 140, 142
processing: automaticity 27, 54, 78, 105; bottom-up 60, 66, 71, 116; control 27, 54, 78, 105; top-down 60, 66, 71
pronouns 13, 87–88, 96, 120–121, 123, 131–132
proper names 114, 119, 121
pros and cons 56–58

quantifiers 143, 145
question words/particles 37, 39, 112

reading: critically 80, 82; post-reading 60, 69, 78, 81–82; pre-reading 60, 69, 78, 81–82; during-reading 60, 69, 78, 81–82
real-life situations 28, 35, 49, 52, 54, 78–79, 100
recasting 38, 42, 45, 47, 73, 112, 132
reconstructing 23, 28, 102, 108, 138
recycling 54, 78, 105, 121

158 Index

rehearsing 41, 46–47, 49, 50–52, 56, 132
repetition 4–6, 9–11, 17, 44–45, 63–64, 71–72, 110
responding 10, 14, 16, 22, 32, 34, 38, 59, 100, 104, 112–113, 116, 139
retelling 79
root 11, 60, 116–118

scaffolding 77, 82
scanning 70
schemata 60
self-confidence 17, 26, 47, 63, 73, 106
sentence: complex 131–132; level 4, 16, 33, 44, 60, 63–64, 68, 86, 88–90, 95, 97–99, 101–102, 111, 120, 125; nominal 121, 124, 130–131; production 33, 44–45, 65, 86, 95; recognition 4, 20, 27, 60; verbal 65–66, 96, 120, 122–123, 131; verbless 65–66, 118, 121–124, 127, 134
shadda 12, 85
sheltering 4
similarities and differences 51, 104–105, 107
skimming 73
social media 57, 82
sound: level 4, 9; production 4, 6; recognition 4, 6, 9–10, 13, 27
speech: direct/indirect 98; level 17; recognition 4
stem sentences/statements 82
stress 10–12
structure: basic 111, 116, 120, 123, 125, 137; complex 33, 54, 84, 105, 137; high frequency 33, 54, 84, 105; low frequency 33, 54, 84, 105
style (writing) 3, 53, 80, 106, 140
summarizing 28, 77–78, 98
supporting opinion 57–59, 82, 109
syllable 11; bi- 11; multi- 11; single 4–5; tri- 11

task 2, 8, 11, 29, 41, 45, 48–49, 86, 100, 108, 138
task-based 49
teaching style 1–2
technology 57, 82
tense: future 126, 135; past 93, 99, 122, 126; present 99, 122, 126, 135
texts: expository 78–79; narrative 47, 51, 78–79, 98–99
topics 2, 27, 29–32, 49–51, 53–54, 56–60, 69, 71, 74–84, 86, 93–94, 97, 99–100, 106–107, 109–110
transforming 28, 47, 98, 129
translating 41–42, 44, 104, 121–122, 135–136

utterance 12–14, 22, 45

verbs 19, 47, 66, 87, 88, 96, 122, 123–129, 131, 134, 142
vocabulary: high frequency 33, 54, 84, 105; key 20, 50, 98, 100, 104, 106–107; low frequency 33, 54, 84; new 20, 30–32, 44–45, 105, 115, 119; specialized 33, 54, 84, 97, 105; *see also* words
vocalizing 131, 143, 145
voice: active 129; passive 129–130, 143, 145
vowels: back 6, 9; front 6, 9; long 5, 10–12, 14; quality 6, 9; short 4, 10–12, 14; *see also* phonemic contrasts

words: boundaries 12; choice 84, 140; key 28, 50, 54, 71–72, 77, 86; level 4, 33, 60, 84–86, 111, 125; meaning 14–15, 31–32, 36, 60–62, 66, 116–118, 142; new 31–32, 66, 71–72, 85; production 4, 6, 33, 84; recognition 4, 13, 17, 20, 27, 60
writing: during drafting 84, 95, 105, 109; post-drafting 84, 95, 105; pre-drafting 84, 95, 105, 109; process 84, 95, 97, 105; product 84

Printed in the United States
by Baker & Taylor Publisher Services